As one of the world's longest established and best-known travel brands, Thomas Cook are the experts in travel.

For more than 135 years our guidebooks have unlocked the secrets of destinations around the world, sharing with travellers a wealth of experience and a passion for travel.

Rely on Thomas Cook as your travelling companion on your next trip and benefit from our unique heritage.

Thomas Cook **traveller** guides

FRENCH ALPS
Thea Macaulay

D1367942

Written by Thea Macaulay
Original photography by Danny Levy Sheehan
Additional research and photography by Xenia Macaulay

Published by Thomas Cook Publishing
A division of Thomas Cook Tour Operations Limited
Company registration no. 3772199 England
The Thomas Cook Business Park, Unit 9, Coningsby Road,
Peterborough PE3 8SB, United Kingdom
Email: books@thomascook.com, Tel: +44 (0) 1733 416477
www.thomascookpublishing.com

Produced by Cambridge Publishing Management Limited
Burr Elm Court, Main Street, Caldecote CB23 7NU
www.cambridgepm.co.uk

ISBN: 978-1-84848-475-7

First edition © 2011 Thomas Cook Publishing
Text © Thomas Cook Publishing
Maps © Thomas Cook Publishing/PCGraphics (UK) Limited

Series Editor: Karen Beaulah
Production/DTP: Steven Collins

Printed and bound in Spain by GraphyCems

Cover photography © Hemis.fr/SuperStock

Contents

Introduction

It is easy to see why the French Alps are such an immensely popular holiday destination. Spectacular landscapes, historic towns, delicious food and an incredible array of sport and leisure activities all contribute to the enduring appeal of this unique corner of France. High mountains contrast with lower hills and valleys to enable the region to cater to an impressive variety of interests year-round, helped by the proximity of the country's dynamic second city, Lyon.

The French Alps are best known for their multitude of renowned ski resorts, and as soon as the snow falls visitors flock to enjoy action-packed holidays in a winter wonderland of towering peaks, beautiful pine forests and breathtaking views. Although undeniably the star of the show, winter is certainly not the only time to visit the mountains. When the snow melts, a whole new world of possibilities opens up. From family-friendly rambles through meadows full of wild flowers to exhilarating land, water and aerial sports, summer in the French Alps is every bit as happening as winter.

Although it is not actually in the Alps, nearby Lyon in the broad Rhône valley is a gateway to the mountains. The largest city in the region, it has distinctive districts, interesting cultural attractions and a well-deserved reputation as the gastronomic capital of the country. Mountain-fringed Grenoble, in the western Alpine area of Isère, is the second-largest city of the region and known as the capital of the Alps. To the northeast, the Haute-Savoie area begins at Lake Geneva (Lac Léman in French) and includes the legendary Alpine giant Mont Blanc. Neighbouring Savoie contains some of Europe's most famous ski areas. The southern Alps are far quieter, but they also have their fair share of beautiful landscapes and outdoor activities.

Designated protected areas, including three national and five regional natural parks, cover a vast amount of the French Alps, providing idyllic hiking territory as well as a haven for wildlife. Animals roaming the mountainsides include hoofed mammals, wolves and smaller mammals. Birds of prey soar overhead, numerous small birds dart about and butterflies hover in the meadows. Conifer forests at low and mid-altitudes give way to Alpine shrubs and tiny flowers higher up. Different ecosystems are found at the region's lakes, which also contribute to the postcard-perfect scenery and offer a range of watersports and boat tours. Besides the almost sea-like Lac Léman (Lake Geneva), Bourget and Annecy are the largest natural lakes, but there are also numerous reservoirs and smaller lakes across the mountains.

Alternative points of interest are provided by the diverse collection of architectural treasures harboured throughout the mountains, the legacy of a fascinating cultural heritage and eventful past. Annecy's enchanting medieval centre and Briançon's fortified Old Town are among the most distinctive urban areas. Scattered across the countryside, eye-catching ruined castles and secluded hilltop villages layer a fairy tale quality on top of the natural marvels of the landscape.

Finally, there is the food and drink: from gourmet dining in Lyon and the region's many gastronomic restaurants to rich and rustic mountain dishes such as fondue, plenty of treats for the taste buds are in store. Animated morning markets, summer café culture and winter après-ski entertainment all enhance the varied experience of the French Alps.

Introduction

The Aiguille du Midi above Chamonix

The land

France's share of the vast Alps, which extend into seven countries, covers a substantial area from Lake Geneva to the Mediterranean coast and includes chains of high and medium mountains as well as lower foothills. From the highest point of Mont Blanc, at 4,810m (15,780ft), down to the deep valleys, this is a land of extremes with natural wonders at every turn and a distinctive ecosystem of flora and fauna.

Landscapes

The captivating landscapes in and around the French Alps are influenced by many features, including altitude, latitude, geological distinctions, rivers and lakes.

Mountains

The Alps have a complex pattern of mountain chains. The highest peaks form a sort of uneven triangle in the centre and east of the region, with the longest edge along the Italian border. Spreading north, west and south of the central massifs, the rest of the range consists of lower peaks, hills and plateaux, collectively known as the Préalpes.

Valleys, lakes and rivers

The largest valley in the region is the verdant Rhône valley, which divides the foothills of the Alps from the hills of Beaujolais and the Ardèche. A wide, flat valley, the Alpine trench, runs between the Préalpes and high peaks. Narrower valleys and river gorges lace the mountains, with streams trickling and waterfalls gushing down the slopes. Lakes vary from large and ecosystem-supporting in the valleys, to tiny and glacial at the summits, and there are also many man-made reservoirs.

Flora

Abundant plants line the lower mountain slopes and valleys. As the altitude increases, the plant life becomes scarcer and more specifically adapted. There are also differences between the northern and southern Alps and between north- and south-facing slopes, adding up to a rich diversity of flora over a relatively small area.

Forests

Conifer forests are a trademark feature of the Alps. Common species are evergreen fir, pine and spruce, all of which thrive at high altitudes, as well as the Mediterranean cypress in the warm

The French Alps

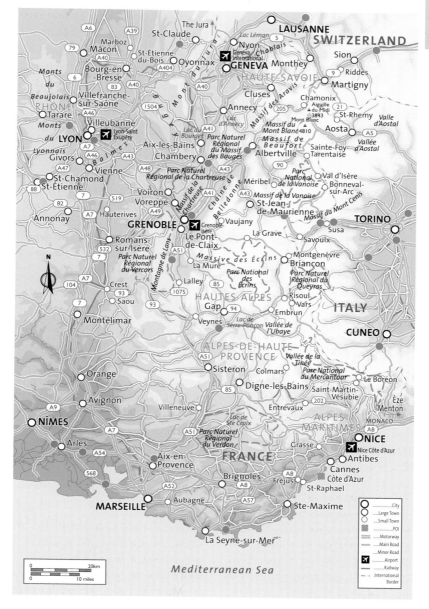

A high mountain waterfall in the Portes du Soleil area

south. Larch, which likes dry, south-facing areas, is the only deciduous conifer in the region, but there are many other deciduous trees, including beech, oak, almond and wild hazel.

Flowers and small plants

From spring through to autumn, an explosion of wild flowers, herbs and berries decorates and scents the mountain countryside. High-altitude Alpine plants have adapted to the harsh conditions above the treeline, which leave them only a brief window of opportunity to grow; most burst into bloom between May and August. Edible wild plants traditionally added to recipes and remedies include wormwood (used in liqueurs), blueberries and dandelion. Keeping up

appearances with their scenic surrounds, many local communities have earned the label of *ville fleurie* or *village fleuri* (town or village in bloom).

Fauna

Like the plants, the animals of the Alps are uniquely suited to this high-altitude environment. The chances of spotting the rarer or more elusive species, particularly the mammals and birds of prey, are greatly increased in the natural parks.

Birds

The sight of a large bird circling the peaks is a mountain classic, and species you might glimpse include golden eagles, bearded vultures and several species of owl (pygmy, Tengmalm's and eagle). Other permanent residents include the ptarmigan, which transforms from bright white in winter to mottled brown in summer, the black grouse and the rock partridge. Numerous migratory birds spend seasons in the mountains. Lakes Geneva, Annecy and Bourget accommodate many aquatic birds, including ducks, swans, gulls and cormorants.

Mammals

A common resident is the Alpine marmot, which roams the high slopes in the summer preparing for winter hibernation. Marmots are typically shy of people, but their loud shrill whistling call makes them easier to locate. Another small inhabitant is the blue (or mountain) hare, which camouflages seasonally by changing from white in winter to brown in summer. Among several species of wild hoofed mammals is the chamois, an agile, adaptive animal with a striped head and small horns. In summer, chamois have a reddish coat, but their thicker winter coats are much darker. Also negotiating the rocky terrain are the moufflon (wild sheep) and the ibex, or bouquetin (wild goat), which both have large, curved horns giving them distinctive silhouettes.

Other wildlife
The big lakes are rich in fish, as are many of the mountain rivers; common species include perch and trout. A diverse insect population includes noisy crickets, grasshoppers and hundreds of butterfly species. Black salamanders are a rare but distinctive resident of some of the nature reserves.

Agriculture
Farming and forestry have influenced the landscape for centuries, but the Alpine agriculture industry has diversified with the times. The traditional dairy and sheep farms have been joined by a variety of crops across the region, from nuts and cereals to olives and lavender. However, the sight of sheep, goats or cows grazing the high pastures, often accompanied by the chiming of bells, is still a characteristic aspect of the mountain landscape.

Cows graze the high pastures during summer

History

6th–5th centuries BC	Celtic tribes settle in the Alps, building cities between the Rhône and Lake Geneva.
218 BC	Hannibal crosses the Alps with his men and elephants.
125–121 BC	The Romans colonise southern France (Gaul).
43 BC	The Romans build Lugdunum, which later becomes Lyon.
AD **313**	Christianity, which has become widespread across the region, is recognised by Emperor Constantine.
476	The Roman Empire falls.
6th–10th centuries	The region is invaded by tribes from the east, including the Franks. Their influence shapes the development of Alpine traditions.
11th–14th centuries	The Alps are divided between the houses of Savoie (also spelt Savoy), Dauphiné and Provence. Feuds, occupations and changing allegiances between the houses, France and Italy continue for centuries.
1232	Chambéry is made capital of Savoie.
1339	Humbert II develops a university in Grenoble.
1349	Humbert II sells Dauphiné to the king of France. The heir to the French throne is given the title of 'dauphin' ('dolphin') and becomes the new ruler of Dauphiné.
1419	Savoie is unified with Piedmont (now in Italy).
1447	The Parliament of Grenoble is created by the dauphin (the future King Louis XI).
Late 15th century	Lyon prospers as a centre for the publishing and textiles industries. Over the following centuries the city becomes particularly renowned for silk-weaving.
1494–1559	During the Italian Wars, Savoie is occupied by France for 23 years.

1559	Savoie regains autonomy and Turin becomes the new capital.
1562–98	The Wars of Religion rage between Catholics and Protestants.
1786	Jacques Balmat and Michel-Gabriel Paccard are the first climbers to reach the summit of Mont Blanc.
1789	The French Revolution begins on 14 July.
1860	Savoie becomes part of France and is divided into the *départements* of Savoie and Haute-Savoie.
1868	Hydroelectricity is used in the French Alps for the first time.
1872	The Fréjus railway tunnel is opened.
1895	The first moving picture is shot in Lyon by the Lumière brothers.
1901	French downhill skiing is born when some Alpine troops in Montgenèvre demonstrate its effectiveness to their bosses. A couple of years later, the first French ski school is founded.
1924	Chamonix hosts the first Winter Olympics.
1940–45	During World War II, the French Alps become a major Resistance stronghold, with fighting particularly concentrated in the Vercors and Haute-Savoie.
1955	The long-anticipated cable-car route between Chamonix and the Aiguille du Midi (3842m/12,600ft) is completed.
1963	The Parc National de la Vanoise, the first national park in France, is created.
1965	The Mont Blanc road tunnel is opened.
1968	Grenoble hosts the 10th Winter Olympics.
1980	The Fréjus road tunnel is opened.
1992	Albertville hosts the 16th Winter Olympics.
2010	Savoie and Haute-Savoie celebrate 150 years of being part of France.

Politics

France is divided into 22 regions, which in turn are subdivided into départements *(smaller administrative regions). The French Alps straddle the regions of Rhône-Alpes and Provence-Alpes-Côte d'Azur. Administrative powers and decisions are divided between national, regional and local levels, and since the 1980s a gradual process of decentralisation has seen increasing delegation of responsibility.*

Administrative regions

Most of the areas covered by this book are in the region of Rhône-Alpes, including the Alpine *départements* of Isère, Savoie and Haute-Savoie, as well as Lyon in the *département* of Rhône. The Lyon and Rhône chapter strays slightly into the northern Rhône-Alpes *département* of Ain, while the Grenoble and Isère chapter includes part of the Drôme *département*. In the southern Alps, the *départements* of Hautes-Alpes, Alpes-de-Haute-Provence and Alpes-Maritimes are under the administration of the Provence-Alpes-Côte d'Azur region.

Political history

With a large part of the French Alps (present-day Savoie and Haute-Savoie) independent until 1860, the political history of the area has followed a unique course. Although Dauphiné became part of France long before Savoie, it retained some autonomy. One of the political events thought to have foretold the French Revolution took place in Grenoble and nearby Vizille in 1788 when an influential group of Grenoble residents staged active and successful protests over the king's planned closure of the local parliament. The Revolution saw the creation of the *départements*, with a *conseil général* (general council) for each one. Dauphiné was split in three, becoming Isère, Drôme and Hautes-Alpes.

Present government

Today, each region has a regional council, led by a president, which heads up the general councils of the *départements*, each with their own local presidents. Under the general councils are municipal councils and mayors for each commune within the *département*.

Economy

The modern economic growth of the French Alps owes a great deal to tourism. Until the 1930s, many young people from the region had been forced to emigrate seasonally or permanently in order to make a living. The development of ski stations turned this around and winter sports now account for a large chunk of the economy. In Savoie and Haute-Savoie, it is estimated that around 40 per cent of local income is now generated by activities based on the snow, which is aptly sometimes called 'white gold'. Meanwhile, national parks and nature reserves have boosted the development of summer tourism. The other main sources of revenue contrast strikingly with each other: high-tech industries such as electrical engineering, fuelled by hydroelectric energy, are major earners for the region, but agriculture continues to make a significant contribution as well.

Topical issues

Topics high on the agenda for the communities of the French Alps include issues of national significance and others that are unique to the mountains. Grenoble, which has a relatively young multicultural population, has seen some headline-worthy responses to state policies and actions. On a regional level, balancing economic development with the preservation of a fragile environment is a key concern. An early example of local communities rising to the ecological challenge was the massive lake clean-up operation organised by the local authorities around Lac d'Annecy in the 1950s. Today, local authorities and mountain businesses across the region are introducing and committing to various environmental initiatives.

Politics

A Resistance memorial outside Briançon town hall

Culture

In the past there were several distinctive cultures within the French Alps and elements of these remain or are remembered in museums. Architecture is a cultural highlight (see pp16–17), influenced by the area's history and geography. There is also a great literary heritage associated with the Alps. The prevailing culture throughout the region today is in tune with the rest of France, with fantastic modern art and performance venues in the towns and cities.

Art and crafts

Art galleries in Lyon and Grenoble exhibit fine collections of classic and modern European art and there are smaller contemporary galleries elsewhere. Local artistic heritage is explored in some museums, notably the Château d'Annecy. Wood was the obvious material of choice for Alpine craftsmen and a number of different woodwork traditions developed. Earthenware (*faïence*), another traditional craft, thrived in the Provence Alps. Throughout the region there are examples of religious art from different periods, including colourful murals dating from the 14th and 15th centuries.

Cinema

Lyon's cinematic heritage, as the setting for the first-ever motion picture, *La Sortie des Usines Lumière* ('Employees Leaving the Lumière Factory'), is showcased with classic film screenings at Hangar du Premier Film, the first-ever set (*see pp38–9*). Various film festivals take place each year in Lyon, Grenoble and Annecy, the latter hosting an annual celebration of animated films. Cinemas across the region show the latest offerings from the flourishing French film industry, as well as international selections.

Folklore and legend

In this land of natural wonders, it is no great surprise that people once believed they shared the mountains with supernatural beings. Until the era of exploration began in the 18th century, residents of the Chamonix valley called Mont Blanc the *montagne maudite* (accursed mountain). Of many European legends about the fairy Mélusine, Sassenage, near Grenoble, has a version involving its local caves. People in Haute-Provence also believed that some rocks were inhabited by fairies, while the Haute-Maurienne village of Bessans had devil stories. The superstitious and pagan beliefs of the past, combined with aspects of

Catholicism, gave rise to an eclectic collection of local festivals, and many are still celebrated today.

Literature

Novelist Stendhal (real name Henri Beyle, *see p50*), born and raised in Grenoble, was the most famous writer from the region, but the evocative scenery of the French Alps has inspired many other literary souls. Among them were the 18th-century writer and philosopher Jean-Jacques Rousseau, who lived at Annecy and Chambéry for some years, and the Romantic poet Alphonse de Lamartine, who wrote *Le Lac* after a doomed love affair at Aix-les-Bains.

Music

Jazz is a musical highlight, celebrated during famous annual festivals in Grenoble and Vienne and performed in a number of bars. Many mountain resorts feature musical events during the ski season, and summer sees outdoor concerts across the region. Traditional music is played at folkloric festivals. Radio stations (which are numerous) play a combination of traditional French songs and popular modern music.

Theatre and dance

Lyon, Grenoble, Annecy, Chambéry and Briançon all have interesting theatres and performance venues. Open-air shows and dances are also staged in various settings during the summer months, particularly as part of annual festivals. The emphasis ranges from local and classical to international performance styles.

Culture

Women in traditional costumes celebrate the Fête du Reblochon in La Clusaz

Alpine architecture

Distinctive architecture is a hallmark cultural feature of the French Alps. From wooden chalets to ruined castles, many of the buildings have become synonymous with the mountainous landscape and contribute substantially to its charm. Although there is a huge amount of diversity throughout the region, the traditional architecture can be divided into broad categories, with grand structures at one end of the spectrum, historic city centres somewhere in the middle and rural houses at the other end. Modern, sometimes controversial, dimensions have been added by purpose-built mountain resorts and contemporary urban designs.

The grand structures of the French Alps include a liberal sprinkling of castles and forts. Most imagination-capturing are the castles dating from the feudal era when aristocratic dynasties were fighting over the land. Many of the châteaux built between the 11th and 14th centuries are now in ruins or include large sections that were rebuilt during later periods. However, their turreted outlines, usually majestically crowning hilltops, still convey an aura of medieval mystique. While castles were mainly residential, forts served a defensive purpose and were constructed in response to continuing territorial disputes and invasion threats. Grenoble's Fort de la Bastille and Sisteron's citadel are surviving examples of town fortifications, but the most remarkable were designed by the prolific military engineer Vauban (see p113).

Religious architecture accounts for many of the historic buildings across the French Alps. Many of the rural churches and chapels are very small and simplistic, but a mixture of influences contributed to the development of ever-grander styles. The oldest churches date from the Italian-inspired Romanesque architectural period of the 11th to 13th centuries, characterised by a spacious but minimalist style. Flamboyant Gothic architecture, a 15th-century French development, ushered in a new era of more elaborate churches, with sculpted stone decorations and stained-glass windows. In 17th-century Savoie, Baroque architecture, another Italian import, satisfied a local desire for increasingly ornamental places of worship. Churches from this period are crammed with paintings, sculptures and gilded details.

Large-scale designs aside, for many people the simple chalet is the most emblematic Alpine building. Classic rural houses, built to deal with the challenges of the mountain climate, vary in style between areas, although there are commonalities. Overhanging roofs protect the houses from snow, balconies create sheltered sunny spots, and large storage areas enable the stockpiling of wood and supplies. The traditional building materials are wood, stone and tiles, which are used in differing quantities across the region. Houses in lower-altitude villages typically contain a higher proportion of wood, while those of the high mountains use more stone.

In the 20th century, a new category of Alpine architecture was created in the form of purpose-built ski resorts. Decades of different building styles and constant expansion proved a hit-and-miss combination, which was unfortunately sometimes more of a recipe for awkward blights on the landscape than architectural harmony with the mountains. However, many of the resorts that did not place a high value on aesthetics at first have begun to turn things around, with creative projects that combine traditional chalet-style architecture with original contemporary designs. A trend for preserving the rustic mountain heritage has led to a number of attractive old buildings, such as Savoyard farmhouses, being transformed into hotels and restaurants.

A traditional Alpine chalet in Morzine

Festivals and events

There is certainly no shortage of festival spirit in the French Alps. Events featuring on the national cultural calendar line up alongside local craft fairs and celebrations of regional heritage, traditions and produce. Many of the villages have their own unique events. Meanwhile, numerous sporting competitions are hosted in the mountains throughout the year, showing a different side to the French Alps.

There are too many events to list them all, but a selection of cultural, gastronomic and sporting fixtures is included here.

January
Concours de Sculptures sur Glace, Valloire

This three-day ice sculpture competition enables visitors to watch sculptors at work.
Tel: (04) 79 59 03 96. www.valloire.net

February–March
Carnaval Vénitien, Annecy

Every year in late February or early March the streets of Annecy are filled with people in traditional masked Venetian costumes.
Tel: (04) 50 52 93 31.
www.lac-annecy.com

March–April
Jazz Grenoble

This two-week festival attracts some big names in international jazz.
Tel: (04) 76 51 65 32.
www.jazzgrenoble.com (in French).

June
Estivales du Château des Ducs, Chambéry

Three weeks of evening performances in front of the castle feature classical and world music, theatre, opera and dance.
Tel: (04) 79 70 63 55. www. estivalesduchateau.com (in French).

June–July
Les Nuits de Fourvière, Lyon

The Gallo-Roman amphitheatres of Lyon provide a dramatic setting for this festival of theatre, films, dance and music.
Tel: (04) 72 57 15 40.
www.nuitsdefourviere.fr (in French).

July
Fêtes de l'Edelweiss, Les Arcs and Bourg-Saint-Maurice

This international folklore festival includes street and bar entertainments.
www.lesarcs.com

Les Noctibules, Annecy

A four-night festival of street arts takes place in the Old Town and at the lakeside. *Tel: (04) 50 33 44 11.*

Tour de France

Spectators line the streets during the Alpine stages of the epic race. *www.letour.fr*

Fête de la Bastille

14 July is the day that launched the French Revolution and it is a public holiday with celebrations across the country.

August

Fête des Guides, Chamonix

The renowned Compagnie des Guides officially inaugurates members with a party of fireworks, displays and concerts on 15 August. *Tel: (04) 50 53 00 88. www.fetedesguides.com (in French).*

Fête du Lac, Tignes

Also on 15 August, this is a day of varied festivities culminating in a fireworks display. *Tel: (04) 79 40 25 80. www.tignes.net*

Corso de la Lavende, Digne-les-Bains

A five-day celebration of all things lavender related. *Tel: (04) 92 36 62 62. www.cdf-digneslesbains.fr (in French).*

Fête du Reblochon et de l'Artisanat, La Clusaz

Folkloric dances accompany this one-day celebration of local cheese and bread production. *Tel: (04) 50 32 65 00. www.laclusaz.com*

October

La Semaine du Goût

'Tasting Week' is a big event across France. It features workshops, cookery demonstrations and restaurant deals. *www.legout.com (in French).*

November

Beaujolais Nouveau

On the third Thursday of the month, street parties mark the release of this famous wine from the cellars.

December

Boarderweek, Val Thorens

Competitions by snowboarders and skiers are accompanied by concerts and other entertainments in this celebration of winter sports. *Tel: (04) 79 00 08 08. www.valthorens.com*

Fête des Lumières, Lyon

Across the city around 8 December, the hugely popular 'Festival of Lights' sees windows lit with candles and public buildings with sound and light shows. *Tel: (04) 72 77 69 69. www.fetedeslumieres.lyon.fr*

Critérium International de la Première Neige, Val d'Isère

The first downhill ski race of the season. *Tel: (04) 79 60 06 60. www.valdisere.com*

Marchés de Noël

In the run-up to Christmas there are festive markets in many towns.

Highlights

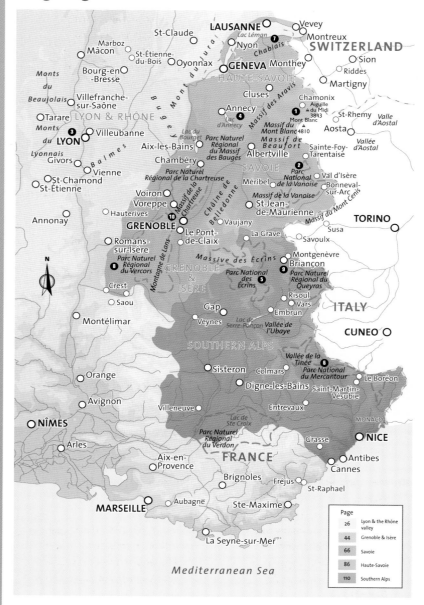

❶ Chamonix-Mont Blanc
Admiring the most spectacular mountains in the Alps, in particular eternally white Mont Blanc, from the famous Aiguille du Midi viewpoint (*see p86*).

❷ Massif de la Vanoise
Skiing or snowboarding a seemingly endless choice of slopes at one of several vast ski areas, while taking in the spectacular scenery of the Vanoise (*see p23*).

❸ Lyon
Dining out in style in France's leading gastronomic city after a packed day of sightseeing in the historic districts and varied museums (*see p26*).

❹ Annecy and Lac d'Annecy
Strolling through the cobbled canal-side streets of the 'Venice of the Alps', before taking your pick of boat trips and watersports on the beautiful lake (*see p94*).

❺ Parc National des Écrins
Walking in the dramatic high peaks of the largest national park in France, looking out for Alpine wildlife and witnessing the changes in flora at different altitudes (*see p118*).

❻ Parc National du Mercantour
Leaving civilisation behind to discover the ultimate mountain wilderness, complete with Bronze Age stone engravings and howling wolves (*see p120*).

❼ Lac Léman and the Chablais
Taking a summer holiday by the biggest lake in Europe and heading into the picturesque hills and mountains nearby for a complete change of scenery (*see p99*).

❽ Parc Naturel Régional du Vercors
Exploring the forests, gorges, caves and plateaux of this fascinating natural park; on foot, by car, by bike or on cross-country skis in the winter (*see p54*).

❾ Briançon and Serre-Chevalier
Enjoying the mixture of urban and rural activities provided between the lively fortified Old Town of Briançon and the peaceful mountains of Serre-Chevalier (*see p110*).

❿ Grenoble
Staying in a spirited Alpine city with mountains everywhere you look and a great selection of restaurants and bars for the evenings (*see p44*).

Suggested itineraries

Long weekend

Whirlwind lake and mountain tour, cultural city break or rural retreat, the three short itineraries below each show a very different side to the region.

Annecy and Chamonix

This long weekend could be fitted into three days, although four would be ideal. A full day in Annecy will enable you to explore the Old Town in the morning and take an afternoon boat trip on the lake. There are train services between Annecy and Chamonix, but if you are driving, take a detour via the Col des Aravis for a stunning view. In Chamonix, go up to the Aiguille du Midi, ride the Montenvers railway to the Mer de Glace and use one of the other cable cars to gain access to stunning high-mountain walking routes. Both towns are lively in the evenings, with plenty of restaurant and bar options.

Lyon

Lyon makes a well-rounded city-break destination. Allow the best part of a day to explore the Vieux Lyon and Fourvière area. Take the funicular up to Fourvière hill for an amazing view over the city, wander through the charming Old Town (stopping for a leisurely lunch) and cross the Saône to reach the city centre (Presqu'île). Spend a second day exploring the Presqu'île and historic Croix Rousse district, as well as strolling along the Rhône riverside and

Annecy, often described as 'the Venice of the Alps'

Pristine snow in Tignes

unwinding in the Parc de la Tête d'Or. For a relaxing day in the countryside, consider a tour of the beautiful Beaujolais wine region. Make the most of Lyon's exceptional culinary scene by discovering a different restaurant each evening.

Alpes-Maritimes

With Nice as an arrival and departure point you can see the remote Mercantour area in a long weekend and also stop off at the beach. The villages of Saint-Martin-Vésubie and Saint-Étienne-de-Tinée are good bases for walking in the national park. Both can be reached within a couple of hours' drive of Nice and there are also some bus services. On returning to Nice, visit the enchanting medieval village of Èze, as well as Nice's own Old Town.

One week

The French Alps are full of single resorts where visitors can stay happily occupied for a winter or summer week, but a week is also long enough to branch out and see more places.

Vanoise ski tour

This itinerary could be managed by taking the ski train directly to Bourg-Saint-Maurice and using local bus networks, although renting a car would allow more flexibility. With Bourg-Saint-Maurice or Les Arcs (Paradiski) as your base, you will be right in the heart of the Vanoise area. Paradiski five- and six-day lift passes include Les Arcs and La Plagne as well as an optional day in one of the Espace Killy resorts and an optional day in the Three Valleys. For a change from skiing, try a day of alternative activities, such as snowshoe walking or sledging.

Lakes and peaks

From Geneva, head for Évian-les-Bains via the medieval lakeside village of Yvoire. After a sleepover in Évian, visit nearby Thonon-les-Bains, before driving inland through the lovely Chablais area. Stop off at the fascinating Gorges du Diable, then continue to Morzine to spend a couple of days walking or mountain biking in the Portes du Soleil. The next stop is Chamonix, with a potential detour en route via lovely Samoëns. After exploring the Mont Blanc area, wrap up the trip with a day or two in Annecy (*see the first long-weekend itinerary*).

Two weeks

In two weeks you can cover a larger part of the Alps and experience contrasting landscapes and activities.

Summer in Serre-Chevalier

Winter wonderland

With Grenoble as a base for the first week, day trips throughout Isère enable you to sample a range of activities. Try snowshoe walking in the Chartreuse, cross-country skiing in the Vercors and downhill skiing at Chamrousse, Les Sept Laux, Les Deux Alpes or Alpe d'Huez. In Grenoble, head up to the Fort de la Bastille for views over the city and mountains. A longer day trip to Chamonix is also feasible and on a clear day well worth it for the unforgettable Aiguille du Midi. For the second week, transfer to Savoie for more serious skiing possibilities in one of the Vanoise areas (Les Trois Vallées, Espace Killy or Paradiski).

La Route des Grandes Alpes

This famous route, marked by road signs, presents an array of possibilities in terms of where to stop off and for how long. Start at Thonon-les-Bains on the shore of Lac Léman. Continue to Morzine and spend some time there. Drive over the Col des Gets and Col de la Colombière then through Le Grand Bornand. From here, the main route continues over the Col des Aravis, but a detour via Annecy is worthwhile. After a short stay in Annecy, loop back round to the main route via the picturesque Massif des Bauges. The route takes in yet more lovely countryside as it traverses the Beaufortain before reaching Bourg-Saint-Maurice. It then continues to Tignes and Val d'Isère, either of which would be a good place to bed down for a while, before going over the Col de l'Iseran, through the Maurienne valley and over the Col du Télégraphe. Passing through Valloire and over the Col du Galibier, the route meanders to Serre-Chevalier and Briançon (a good stopover point). Continue to Guillestre and take the optional detour to the Lac de Serre-Ponçon, a relaxing place to stay. From Barcelonette, opt for the Col de la Bonette and the route through the Mercantour, where you can enjoy walks away from the beaten track. The final section descends to the coast, ending at the seaside resort of Menton. For full route details, see

www.grande-traversee-alpes.com

Longer: embellishing the Route des Grandes Alpes

Having more than two weeks to devote to your Alpine experience provides a golden opportunity to add an extension to the epic tour. Start at Lyon, instead of Thonon-les-Bains, and explore the city before heading to the Alps. Drive to Grenoble to spend a night or two and visit the Vercors. Go north via the Chartreuse and Lac du Bourget to the Geneva area and consider a day touring the Jura mountains on the other side of the lake. Loop back around the lake to Thonon-les-Bains to get on to the main route south. Add hiking in the Écrins national park to the route, using either Bourg d'Oisans or Briançon as a base.

The impressive Massif du Mont Blanc

Lyon and the Rhône valley

Famed as a hotbed of gourmet cuisine, Lyon sits harmoniously in the wine-producing Rhône valley. Elegant, historic and vibrant, France's second city is much more than a treat for the taste buds; there is also great art and architecture to feast the eyes upon. The vineyards, rolling hills and stone villages of the surrounding countryside invite summer day trips.

An unusual geography of two rivers, the Rhône and the Saône, and two hills, Fourvière and Croix Rousse, gives Lyon a distinctive and easily navigable layout. Proud of its long-standing annual *fête des lumières*, this attractive city illuminates its monuments each night. In a combined cultural effort, the city's museums provide insights into an enthralling past and also establish a firm place on the contemporary art scene. Meanwhile, architectural heritage abounds, from Roman amphitheatres to the medieval and Renaissance period houses in the wonderfully preserved Old Town. And when it comes to sampling the local cuisine, visitors are truly spoilt for choice.

The landscapes in the Rhône area contrast with and complement the landscapes of the Alps. Wine-rich Beaujolais, with its scenic hills, extends northwest of Lyon alongside the river Saône as far as the border with Burgundy. East of the city the marshy plains of the Dombes present an entirely different landscape, rich in wildlife, while the medieval village of Pérouges is a popular day-trip choice. To the south, the town of Vienne continues the Roman theme, with several superb monuments.

LYON

Lyon has nine *arrondissements* (districts), but the city centre is effectively divided into three main areas by the natural borders of the rivers. On the west of the Saône is the Old Town of Vieux Lyon, overlooked by Fourvière hill. Sandwiched between the rivers is the Presqu'île ('Almost Island'), topped by hilly Croix Rousse. Finally, on the east side of the Rhône are the Rive Gauche (left bank) and an area known as Part-Dieu, after the main train station. Orientation is also helped by the many public squares throughout the city, particularly in the Presqu'île. Maps and information on Lyon's many attractions are provided at the tourist office, which also sells the Lyon City

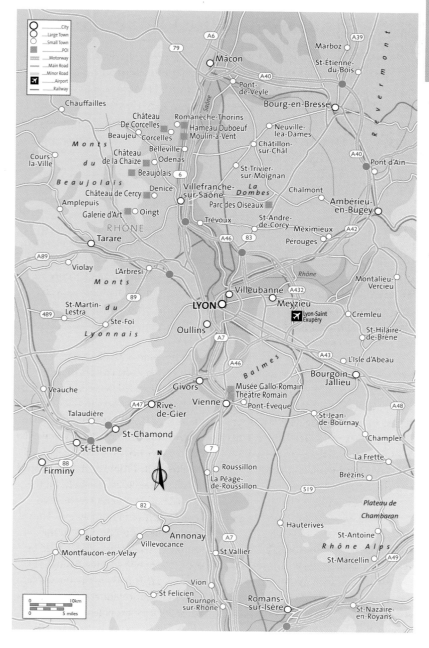

Lyon viewed from Fourvière Hill

Card (one / two / three days – adults €20 / 30 / 40, children aged 4–15 €11.50 / 16.50 / 21.50). The card covers all public transport and museum admissions, as well as guided city and river tours.

Office du Tourisme et des Congrès du Grand Lyon, Place Bellecour. Tel: (04) 72 77 69 69. www.lyon-france.com. Open: 9am–6pm.

Fourvière and Vieux Lyon

This is the oldest section of Lyon and a designated UNESCO World Heritage Site, where the city's layers of history are preserved and displayed. Habitation of Fourvière hill dates from 43 BC when the Romans founded the colony of Lugdunum, capital of the Three Gauls. There are two surviving Roman amphitheatres, but Fourvière's most visible monuments are the basilica and the Tour Métallique, a mini Eiffel Tower which functions as a TV transmitter. Marked walking trails downhill to Vieux Lyon take about 15–20 minutes, ending in the Old Town's cobbled alleys, crammed with restaurants, cafés and shops, interspersed with museums, churches and intriguing architectural features such as the *traboules* (secret passages, *see box opposite*), which link several of the streets.

TRABOULES

Maps from the tourist office show unnamed lines between streets, linking, branching and dead-ending. These curious ancillary avenues are *traboules* and *miraboules* (which end in courtyards), a warren of 315 passages hidden throughout Lyon. Some were created in the Roman era, but most in the 19th century so the *canuts* (silk weavers) could transport silk in bad weather. They were also used by the Resistance in World War II and are still thoroughly functional, whether as shortcuts or entrances to restaurant kitchens and apartment buildings. Push open tall doors, dive down dark arched tunnels past the spiral staircases, glimpse occasional patches of sky far above, and emerge blinking in another place.

Basilique Notre-Dame de Fourvière

Watching over the city from the top of a hill, the grand 19th-century basilica is one of the most iconic features of the Lyon skyline. The palatial interior architecture epitomises the lavish style of the period, with every wall covered in religious scenes created in magnificent gold-studded detail from tiny, shiny mosaic tiles. Before the basilica was built, the site had already been a sanctuary and Fourvière was known as the 'hill of prayer'. The city's famous Fête des Lumières has its origins in the inauguration of a statue of the Virgin Mary at Fourvière chapel on 8 December 1852.
Place de Fourvière. Tel: (04) 78 25 13 01. www.lyon-fourviere.com. Open 8am–7pm.

Cathédrale Saint-Jean

The cathedral's architecture is mixed, with Gothic and Romanesque sections. More than 400 years divide the newest sections, added in the early 16th century, from the oldest, dating from the late 11th century. Inside, the

The Basilique Notre-Dame de Fourvière rises above the city of Lyon

The ornate astronomical clock in Cathédrale St-Jean

architecture is elegant, with touches of colour from stained-glass windows, and an interesting ornately detailed astronomical clock with musical chimes (which ring out every day at noon, 2pm, 3pm and 4pm) worth listening out for.

Place Saint-Jean. Open: Mon–Fri 8am–noon & 2–7.30pm, Sat & Sun 8am–noon & 2–7pm.

Musée d'Art Réligieux (Museum of Religious Art)

Religious art and artefacts connected to the history of the Fourvière basilica are exhibited next door at this elegant museum, also known as the Museum of Sacred Art.

8 place de Fourvière. Tel: (04) 78 25 13 01. Open: Apr–Dec daily 10am–12.30pm & 2–5.30pm. Admission charge.

Musée de la Civilisation Gallo-Romaine (Museum of Gallo-Roman Civilisation)

On the site of the Fourvière amphitheatres, the museum showcases ancient artefacts discovered in and around Lyon.

17 rue Cléberg. Tel: (04) 72 38 39 30. Open: Tue–Sun 10am–6pm. Admission charge (free for under 18s).

Musée Gadagne (Gadagne Museum)

Within this impressive 16th-century mansion house are two museums, covering an unusual combination of the local history of Lyon and the international history of puppets. The Musée des Marionettes du Monde (Museum of World Puppets) tells the story of famous Lyonnais puppet Guignol (*see box opposite*), as well as documenting the development of puppet theatres across the world. Peeping out from the glass display cabinets, the marionettes are amusing, delightful and sometimes surprisingly peculiar. Meanwhile, the Musée d'Histoire de Lyon (Museum of Lyon History) presents a sweeping overview of the city's development from antiquity to today.

Place du Petit Collège. Tel: (04) 78 42 03 61. www.museegadagne.com. Admission charge (free for children, adults under 26 and visitors with disabilities).

GUIGNOL

The turn of the 19th century found Laurent Mourguet – an out-of-work *canut* (silk weaver) – pulling teeth in the local market. He started puppet shows with Polichinelle (Punch) to attract and distract customers, but quit dentistry altogether after inventing the gleefully impertinent and instantly popular character of Guignol, gifted with both his creator's snub nose and his sharp wit. Always poorer yet always smarter than his upper-class opponents, Guignol was variously portrayed as having the professions of his audience – silk weaver, peddler, shoemaker – and Mourguet would incorporate local news and gossip into the act. Guignol swiftly spread around France and today remains a beloved rebel, ever mocking of authority.

Musée des Miniatures et Décors de Cinéma (Museum of Miniatures and Cinema Sets)

One of Lyon's quirkier attractions, this museum has a fascinating collection of models, and demystifies some of the secrets of the special effects used in a selection of well-known films.

60 rue Saint-Jean. Tel: (04) 72 00 24 77. www.mimlyon.com. Open: Mon–Fri 10am–6.30pm, Sat & Sun 10am–7pm. Admission charge.

Théâtres Romains

This open archaeological site, located just a short stroll downhill from the Fourvière basilica, consists of two semi-circular stone amphitheatres that were entertainment venues used by the inhabitants of ancient Lugdunum. The larger amphitheatre dates from around 15 BC, while its smaller neighbour, the Odeon dedicated to music, was built slightly later. Both have well-preserved marble floors, but little else remains beyond the stone-step seating.

The larger of Fourvière's two Roman amphitheatres

Walk: Fourvière and Vieux Lyon

This route weaves a historical path through two of Lyon's most fascinating areas. The walk covers a distance of about 3km (1¾ miles). Allow three or four hours to visit all the sights.

Start at Vieux Lyon Cathédrale St-Jean metro stop (line D). Take the funicular up to Fourvière. The basilica is unmissable.

1 Basilique Notre-Dame de Fourvière

The basilica's white columns and towers are topped by a gilded figure of the Virgin Mary.

2 Panoramic view

There is a fantastic view over the city from behind the basilica.
Below the Place de Fourvière, take Rue Roger Radisson downhill. The archaeological site is a few minutes' walk on the left.

3 Théâtres Romains

Enjoy a different view over the city as you descend the stone steps and look back at the amphitheatres' curved outlines.
You will reach the large theatre first, then the Odeon below on the right. Take the path down, turning right on to Rue de l'Antiquaille. Take the sharp left after Menimes metro stop, then the stairway on your right. Follow the road as it turns into Montée du Gourguillon. At the foot of the hill (Place de la Trinité), turn

right. Turn left on to Avenue de Doyenné and continue to Place Saint-Jean.

4 Cathédrale Saint-Jean

The exterior of the cathedral has intricate carvings. Inside, note the stained-glass windows and the ancient crosses on either side of the altar.
Turn right outside the cathedral and walk up Rue Saint-Jean, one of the main shopping streets of Vieux Lyon. The museum is at No 60.

5 Musée des Miniatures et Décors de Cinéma

There are two miniature sets viewable in the window, and some more miniature exhibits and film models in a free gallery.
A few doors up from the museum, the entrance to the traboule *is at No 54.*

6 The long *traboule*

One of the best *traboules*, it also winds through a courtyard. You will come out at 27 rue du Boeuf.

Turn right and walk straight up. The Musée Gadagne is on your left.

7 Musée Gadagne

The museum showcases an impressive range of international and antique puppets, enhanced through short films and recordings.

Take Rue de la Fronde in front of the museum, turn left at the end and then right towards the river. Turn left through a small square (with picnic benches), to see the mural on the wall in front.

8 Mur de la Cour des Loges

Depicting an Old Town hotel, this is one of Lyon's many fresco paintings.
Take Quai de Bondy north. Cross the river at Passerelle Saint-Vincent. The mural covers the building just across the bridge.

9 Fresque des Lyonnais Célèbres

See how many of the tall building's inhabitants you can identify.
From here, you could continue up to Croix Rousse or into the centre of town.

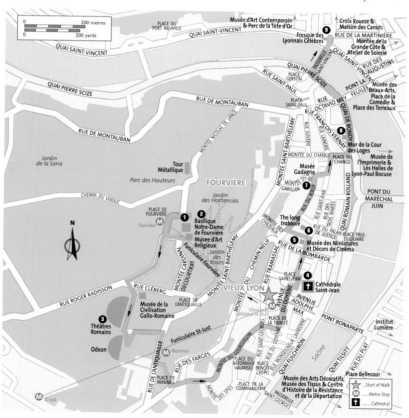

Walk: Fourvière and Vieux Lyon

Presqu'île

The long, thin Presqu'île peninsula at the heart of the city is made up of a grid of streets, punctuated with smart squares and opening out on to the banks of the rivers. North of Place des Terreaux the streets start to climb uphill towards the distinctive Croix Rousse district (*see p36*).

Fresque des Lyonnais Célèbres (Fresco of Famous Lyon Inhabitants)

One of the most impressive and fascinating murals in Lyon, this towering building appears crammed with the city's famous past, present and fictional inhabitants. Residents lingering in the windows and doors include cinema creators Auguste and Louis Lumière, Laurent Mourguet with his puppet Guignol, author Antoine de Saint-Exupéry with his Little Prince, and the famed chef Paul Bocuse. Appropriately, in this city where food itself is a celebrity, the ground floor depicts a painted restaurant so realistic you feel you might wander in off the street for some *andouillette* (local sausage).
Corner of Rue de la Martinière.

Musée des Arts Décoratifs (Decorative Arts Museum)

Next to the Musée des Tissus (*see opposite*), this museum opens a door to the opulent era of 18th-century interior design.
34 rue de la Charité. Tel: (04) 78 38 42 00. www.musee-des-tissus.com. Open: Tue–Sun 10am–noon & 2–5.30pm.

THE URBAN GALLERY

THE URBAN GALLERY

In the 1970s, a group of Lyonnais students decided that art was locked into galleries, invisible to the general public. Their solution was murals, an idea which perfectly coincided with the city revitalisation plans of the mayor at the time, Michel Noir. Over three decades later, there are 180 murals in Lyon, across every district. These *trompe l'œil* masterpieces both mirror and extend the city streets. They remember the past and imagine the future. Formerly grey façades now spring out in vibrant colours. From the 400sq m (4,300sq ft) 'La Bibliothèque de la Cité' mural to myriad amateur frescoes revealed as shutters come down over shopfronts, the idea of art for everyone has been a marked success.

Admission charge (free with Musée des Tissus ticket). Metro: Ampère.

Musée des Beaux-Arts (Fine Arts Museum)

The prestigious Museum of Fine Arts has a wonderful collection of European paintings and sculptures. In addition, the museum exhibits snapshots of artistic traditions from the Middle Ages to the present day, from international antiquities to modern graphic art. There is a café-restaurant, a shop and a lovely garden.
20 place des Terreaux. www.mba-lyon.fr. Open: Wed–Thur & Sat–Mon 10am–6pm, Fri 10.30am–6pm. Metro: Hôtel de Ville.

Musée de l'Imprimerie (Printing Museum)

Exhibitions, animations and workshops at this museum maintain a cultural connection to the technology that significantly aided Lyon's development. *13 rue de la Poulaillerie. Tel: (04) 78 37 65 98. www.imprimerie.lyon.fr. Open: Wed–Sun 9.30am–noon & 2–6pm. Metro: Cordeliers.*

Musée des Tissus (Textile Museum)
Lyonnais silks are the stars of the show at the renowned Textile Museum, but the extensive collections also include fabrics of different periods from across the world, exquisitely woven into tapestries, carpets and garments. *34 rue de la Charité. Tel: (04) 78 38 42 00. www.musee-des-tissus.com. Open: Tue–Sun 10am–5.30pm. Admission charge. Metro: Ampère.*

Place Bellecour
Lyon's largest square, place Bellecour, has as its centrepiece a statue of Louis XIV on horseback. After dark there is a great view of the illuminated Basilique Notre-Dame de Fourvière and the Tour Métallique, with the statue in the foreground.

Place de la Comédie
This central square is dominated by two monumental buildings, the Opéra de Lyon and the Hôtel de Ville (town hall). The opera building is especially eye-catching at night, when it is lit up with a series of red lights behind the columns and statues. On summer evenings free jazz concerts take place

Lyon and the Rhône valley

At night, the buildings along the Rhône are lit up

under the open arches at pavement level (*mid-Jun–mid-Sept 7–11pm*).

Place des Terreaux

On the other side of the Hôtel de Ville is another attractive square, the Place des Terreaux. The square's signature monument is the Fontaine Bartholdi, a huge lead statue depicting a woman (France personified) seated in a chariot pulled by four horses symbolising four rivers. The fountain was sculpted by the famous 19th-century sculptor Frédéric Auguste Bartholdi, best known for designing the Statue of Liberty. Across the square, a more modern piece of fountain art is provided by gushing jets of water that shoot up from the ground.

Croix Rousse

Once home to the *canuts* (silk weavers) of Lyon, Croix Rousse is now an arty neighbourhood dotted with workshops, galleries and boutiques. Access back down to river level from the hill is via a selection of stairways and steep slopes, affording fantastic views over the rooftops. This creative, vibrant district contains the famous Mur des Canuts (*corner of Boulevard des Canuts & Rue Denfert-Rochereau*) as a memento of the area's history.

Atelier de Soierie (Silk Workshop)

Visitors to the atelier can watch artists screen-printing silk items, which are later sold in an on-site shop.
33 rue Romarin. Tel: (04) 72 07 97 83. www.atelierdesoierie.com. Open: Mon–Fri 9am–noon & 2–6pm, Sat 9am–1pm & 2–6pm. Free admission. Metro: Hôtel de Ville.

Maison des Canuts (House of the Silk Weavers)

The fascinating and tragic tale of the *canuts* who shaped the development of Croix Rousse is told at this small

The Fontaine Bartholdi on Place des Terreaux

One of the workshop exhibits at the Maison des Canuts

museum. Visitors can wander freely through several exhibition rooms, or opt for a guided tour to learn more about the weavers' history and see a loom demonstration.

10–12 rue d'Ivry. Tel: (04) 78 28 62 04. www.maisondescanuts.com. Open: Tue–Sat 10am–6pm. Free admission, but charge (except for under 12s) for guided tours: 11am & 3.30pm, mainly in French. Metro: Croix Rousse.

Montée de la Grande Côte

Descending straight down from the top of Croix Rousse to Place des Terreaux, the Montée de la Grande Côte is a steep street but a very scenic pedestrian route. The buildings lining the walkway are typical of the district's architecture and contain a few *traboules*.

Part-Dieu and Rive Gauche

Centre d'Histoire de la Résistance et de la Déportation (Resistance and Deportation History Centre)

This thought-provoking museum is committed to the remembrance of World War II, when Lyon suffered atrocities under Gestapo commander Klaus Barbie, and the French Resistance waged battles in the region.

14 avenue Berthelot. Tel: (04) 78 72 23 11. www.chrd.lyon.fr. Open: Wed–Fri 9am–5.30pm, Sat & Sun 9.30am–6pm. Admission charge (free for under 18s). Metro: Jean Macé. Tram: Centre Berthelot.

Institut Lumière (Lumière Institute)

Made up of a cinema, museum and library, the institute celebrates and showcases Lyon's important connection to cinematic history. Set in the beautiful Art Nouveau villa that was home to the first family of film-making, the Musée Lumière features a treasure trove of exhibits within a maze of rooms. Along the path outside, floor plaques chart the development of cinema from the first 'tricks of the eye' to the fully functional film process. The grounds still house the remains of the factory where the first-ever moving picture was shot, now a cinema (*see p14*).

Rue du Premier-Film. Tel: (04) 78 78 18 95. Open Tue–Sun 11am–6.30pm. Admission charge. Metro: Monplaisir-Lumière.

Les Halles de Lyon-Paul Bocuse (Paul Bocuse Covered Market of Lyon)

This large covered market, which recently added the name of Lyon's most famous chef to its title, provides a truly gastronomic shopping experience. There is an array of cheeses and meats available, as well as various other products. Look out for the delightful vividly coloured cakes and pastries.

Cours Lafayette. Open: Tue–Sat 8am–7pm, Sun 8am–2pm. Metro: Part-Dieu.

Musée d'Art Contemporain (Museum of Contemporary Art)

On the northern edge of the Parc de la Tête d'Or is the thoroughly modern Museum of Contemporary Art. The museum closes briefly in between temporary exhibitions, so it is worth checking the website before visiting.

81 quai Charles de Gaulle. Tel: (04) 72 69 17 17. www.mac-lyon.com. Open: Wed–Fri noon–7pm, Sat & Sun 10am–7pm. Admission charge (free for under 18s).

Parc de la Tête d'Or

The 'Park of the Golden Head' (named after a mysterious artefact that was thought to be buried in the area but

The Parc de la Tête d'Or, Lyon

THE BIRTHPLACE OF CINEMA

The famous (and aptly named) Lumière brothers – Auguste and Louis – were raised in Lyon, working there in their father's photography business. In 1894 Antoine Lumière asked his sons to look at moving pictures. In 1895 they patented their Cinématographe. By 1896 they had started opening 'Cinématographe theatres'. This achievement involved a web of intersecting inventions, from the camera, to the film, to the method of perforation allowing the film to move through camera and projector. Previously, moving images were seen only in the Kinetoscope single-person-view 'peep shows' – but the Lumières envisioned film as a shared pleasure and through technical innovation and business insight they set the fourth art on its proper path.

was never found) is a vast oasis of green within a short distance of the city centre. There is a lake with pedalos, a small zoo, a botanical garden and a tropical house.

RHÔNE
Beaujolais

More reminiscent of the northern Tuscan countryside than the more famous French wine areas, Beaujolais is made up of a patchwork of vineyards and forests spread over rolling hills. Each area has a unique character. Southern Beaujolais is known as the Pierres Dorées ('Golden Stones') area because of the hue of its buildings. The middle section, roughly from Villefranche-sur-Saône to Saint-Étienne-la-Varenne, is called Beaujolais Villages. Finally, the north of the

region is serious wine territory, where the *grands crus*, the highest-quality wines, of Beaujolais are produced. To the west of the vineyards is the forested Vert Beaujolais ('Green Beaujolais'). As well as offering wine-oriented tours, Beaujolais is an ideal destination for cycling and walking, and there are signposted routes and trails across the region.

Beaujeu

This small town is a good place to organise an independent trip around Beaujolais, as the tourist office can provide information on wine cellars, walking and biking routes.
Office de Tourisme, Place de l'Hôtel de Ville: Tel: (04) 74 69 22 88. www.aucoeurdubeaujolais.fr. Open: Mar–Apr & Oct–Nov Wed–Sun 10am–noon & 2.30–6pm; Jun–Sept 9.30am–12.30pm & 2.30–6.30pm.

Château de Cercy

This is not actually a castle, but the home of the Picards, a family of *viticulteurs* who welcome visitors at their pretty winery. They have maintained a lovely old cellar, which they open for visits. Wines tasted here demonstrate the ever-improving quality of Beaujolais wine.
Cercy, Denicé. Tel: (04) 74 67 34 44. Free admission, but charge for tour groups.

Château de la Chaize

The vast wine estate (the largest in Beaujolais) of this 16th-century castle

produces Brouilly. As well as tasting the wine, visitors can explore the 200-year-old massive vaulted cellar running the 108m (355ft) length of the building.
La Chaize, Odenas. Tel: (04) 74 03 41 05. www.chateaudelachaize.com. Open: daily. Admission charge.

Château de Corcelles
In the heart of the *grands crus* region, the medieval castle at Corcelles makes an interesting brief stop. Parts of the castle date from the 13th century, others from the 15th.
Tel: (04) 74 66 00 24. Open: Apr–Oct Mon–Sat 10am–6.30pm, Nov–Mar Mon–Sat 10am–noon & 2.30–5.30pm. Free admission.

Hameau Duboeuf
Combining railway culture with viticulture, this unusual centre includes a large museum dedicated to the history of Beaujolais and wine production set in a converted train station. The exhibits cover every aspect of wine production, right down to the art of cork making. Wine tastings are offered in a beautiful dining/function room styled as a station salon from the turn of the 20th century.
La Gare, Romanèche-Thorins. Tel: (03) 85 35 22 22. www.hameauduvin.com. Open: Apr–Oct Mon–Sat 9am–7pm, Nov–Mar Mon–Sat 10am–6pm. Admission charge (free for under 16s).

Moulin-à-Vent
Having given its name to one of the *grands crus*, this 15th-century windmill has become a signature Beaujolais monument. Opposite is a wine cooperative offering tastings and selling bottles from numerous local producers.
Union de Viticulteurs Moulin à Vent, Romanèche-Thorins. Tel: (03) 85 35 59

Sunflowers add an extra splash of colour to the countryside around Lyon

39. *www.moulin-a-vent.net.*
Admission charge.

10am–5.30pm (last admission 4.30pm).
Admission charge.

Oingt

This especially pretty golden stone village splendidly showcases southern Beaujolais architecture. A wander down the little main street leads to narrow side streets to explore and lovely hilltop views to admire. Several artists have set up shop here selling ceramics, jewellery and paintings. Weekend afternoons are the best time to find all the shops open, although the **Galerie d'Art** (*Tel: (04) 72 52 96 75*) is open Tuesday to Sunday.

La Dombes

Spreading across the northern Rhône valley like a patchwork quilt of shallow lakes and marshy farmland, La Dombes is an excellent region for spotting birds, from stork to osprey, sandpiper to nightingale. Birdwatching walking routes are listed on *http://ladombes.free.fr*, and it is also worth seeking out a knowledgeable local guide. The site *www.birdingpal.org* can put visitors in touch with a birdwatcher from the area.

Parc des Oiseaux

Adding considerably to the area's many bird inhabitants, the Parc des Oiseaux is home to an international array of winged species.
Tel: (04) 74 98 05 54.
www.parcdesoiseaux.com. Open: Jul–Aug 9.30am–8pm (last admission 6.30pm); Apr–Jun & Sept 9.30am–7pm (last admission 6pm); Mar & Oct–Nov

Pérouges

Thanks to bus services from the Gare de Perrache in Lyon, the popular medieval village of Pérouges can easily be visited on a day trip from the city. The village's appeal resides in its charming yellow-stone and timber houses, cobblestone lanes and general sense of days gone by.

Vienne

Visitors interested in Roman architecture can take an excursion to Vienne, an old Gallo-Roman town 30km (19 miles) south of Lyon. Vienne's heritage is spread over several sites. Standing proud in the centre of town (in the Place Charles de Gaulle), the Temple d'Auguste et de Livie is a wonderfully intact rectangular structure of Corinthian columns topped with a roof, while a hillside amphitheatre, the **Théâtre Romain**, overlooks the town (*Rue du Cirque. Tel: (04) 74 85 39 23. Open: Apr–Aug daily & Sept–Oct Tue–Sun 9.30am–1pm & 2–6pm; Nov–Mar Tue–Sat 9.30am–12.30pm & 2–5pm, Sun 1.30–5.30pm. Admission charge*). The rest of the excavated Gallo-Roman ruins have been turned into the **Musée Gallo-Romain**, a museum site at Saint-Romain-en-Gal, just across the river from Vienne (*2 chemin de la Plaine Gal. Tel: (04) 74 53 74 01. www.musees-gallo-romains.com. Open: Tue–Sun 10am–6pm. Admission charge*).

Wines from the hills

Compared to regions like Bordeaux, Burgundy and Champagne, the Rhône-Alpes is not widely renowned for wine production, yet parts of this mountainous area harbour surprisingly fruitful vineyards. Beaujolais and Savoie produce some great wines, many of which are only or mainly sold locally, providing pleasant discoveries for visiting wine drinkers. Beaujolais may be best known for the Beaujolais Nouveau ceremoniously released from the cellars every November, but there is much more to the story of this unique wine area.

The majority of Beaujolais wines are red and made from a single grape variety, the Gamay noir à jus blanc, although there are a few whites (Chardonnay) and rosés. Despite the uniformity of the grapes, variations in the soil and production styles throughout the area lead to a surprisingly diverse collection of wines.

Part of Beaujolais' charm is that there are very few large-scale producers. Instead, hundreds of vineyards run by families and small companies are scattered throughout the hills. This means that visitors are spoilt for choice over where to taste and buy wine, with caves (wine cellars) everywhere. One way to navigate the caves is to go on a guided tour; especially helpful for non-French-speaking visitors. Individualised itineraries with a knowledgeable English-speaking guide can be arranged through Lyon-based company **Excelys Tours** (see p172).

There are ten *grands crus* produced in the north of the area, each named after a small locality or village. From south to north, these are: Brouilly, Côte de Brouilly, Régnié, Morgon, Chiroubles, Fleurie, Moulin-à-Vent, Chénas, Juliénas and Saint-Amour. Literally translated as 'great growths', *grands crus* are the most distinguished wines. In contrast to the autumn youngsters, the *crus*, which are considered to improve with maturity, are typically not drunk until the following spring and are often left for several years to develop into vintages. In the central heartland of the area, Beaujolais-Villages wines are produced, while straightforward Beaujolais, including Beaujolais Nouveau, hails from the southern 'Golden Stone' area.

In Savoie, grapes are cultivated from Lac Léman to the Massif des

Bauges and Isère valley. Vineyards may not seem an obvious choice for a mountain region, but the history of Savoie wines dates from Roman times, making them a long-standing aspect of the landscape and culture. Today, a number of Vins de Savoie carry the prestigious Appellation d'Origine Contrôlée (AOC; 'label of inspected origin'), a guarantee of quality that means they have met an exacting set of standards. Like those of Beaujolais, Savoie's vineyards are mainly small and set in scenic sloping countryside. Unlike in Beaujolais, there are several different grape varieties here and the majority of wines produced are white. La Combe de Savoie, in the Isère valley south of Albertville, is the most wine-rich area and the birthplace of several dry whites, including the interestingly named Apremont ('Bitter Mountain') and Abymes ('Chasms'). The upper Rhône valley, north of Lac du Bourget, is the second main vineyard area. Wines produced here include the sweeter Roussette de Savoie, as well as one of the few reds, Gamay de Chautagne. There are a few vineyards in the Massif des Bauges, where another red, Mondeuse, is produced. Finally, sheltering in the warmer climate of the Lac Léman area is another batch of productive vineyards. The Château de Ripaille (*see p100*) near Thonon-les-Bains sits at the heart of a wine-making estate.

An old-style Beaujolais wine cellar

Grenoble and Isère

In a curious twist of geography, the 'capital' of the French Alps is also the flattest city in France. Grenoble's snug position at the meeting of the Isère and Drac rivers, enveloped by sharply rising mountain peaks, provides magnificent views and easy access to the Alpine countryside. At the heart of the historic Dauphiné region, the département *of Isère features numerous scenic and sporting highlights within its gentle hills and high mountains.*

Grenoble has two regional natural parks on its doorstep: the Chartreuse to the north, and the Vercors to the west and southwest. Looming large to the east of the city is the attention-grabbing Chaîne de Belledonne. The family-friendly ski resorts of Chamrousse and Sept Laux are located here, comfortably within day-trip distance of Grenoble. Southern Isère boasts some beautiful scenery, particularly around the route from Grenoble to Gap. The region's most extensive ski areas are the popular resorts of L'Alpe d'Huez and Les Deux Alpes, which are located in the Oisans area in the southeast. Near these ski areas is the high-altitude Massif des Écrins, much of which is protected within the Parc National des Écrins (*see p118*).

Adventurous sports are big in Isère as throughout the Alps, but this is also a region of more leisurely activities. The Vercors and Chartreuse are great locations for lower-altitude walking and driving excursions and there are other attractions near Grenoble as well, such as the Laffrey lakes (Lacs de Laffrey). Grenoble itself, although typically seen more as a place to pass through than to stay, has several interesting museums and a cable car up to a hilltop fort with fantastic views of the valley and mountains. Plentiful restaurants and a vibrant nightlife add to the appeal of spending some time in the city.

GRENOBLE

Grenoble is a thriving modern city with a long history, which is documented in the museums. Although a town had been established on the site by the ancient Gauls and extended by the Romans under the name of Gratianopolis, Grenoble was really developed under the House of Dauphiné. The last independent dauphin founded the first university in the city shortly before selling the province to France. Today, Grenoble has several universities and a large student population, which contributes to a lively atmosphere and buzzing nightlife.

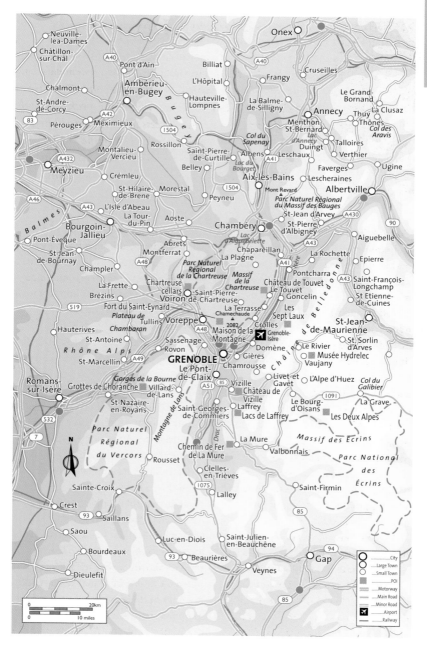

The city has also been shaped by various industries over the years and is now a centre of technology. However, with the industrial areas concentrated in the suburbs, central Grenoble has kept its distinctive heritage and fresh Alpine feel, helped of course by the views and the crisp mountain air. For city information, visit the **Office de Tourisme** in the Maison du Tourisme (*14 rue de la République. Tel: (04) 76 42 41 41. www.grenoble-tourisme.com*).

Old Town

Grenoble's Old Town is an interesting jumble of narrow streets and elegant squares, with architecture from various historical periods. Medieval, Gothic and Renaissance styles are all represented.

Cathédrale Notre-Dame and Musée de l'Ancien Évêché (Museum of the Former Bishops' Palace)

Place Notre-Dame is the site of the only accessible Gallo-Roman ruins in Grenoble. Sections from the ancient

The Isère river flowing through Grenoble

walls of Gratianopolis discovered under the square can be visited at an archaeological site in the basement of the Musée de l'Ancien Évêché, attached to the cathedral. This former palace was home to the bishops of the city for over 500 years. Alongside the Roman walls in the museum basement is a 4th-century baptistery. Above ground, permanent and temporary exhibits focus on the cultural and industrial history of Isère. The carefully restored cathedral is the most dominating structure above ground.

Musée de l'Ancien Évêché, 2 rue Très-Cloîtres. Tel: (04) 76 03 15 25. www.ancien-eveche-isere.fr. Open: Mon & Wed–Sat 9am–6pm, Tue 1.30–6pm, Sun 10am–7pm. Free admission.

Place Grenette

At the edge of the Old Town, cheerful Place Grenette is a popular meeting spot and the ideal location to experience French café culture at one of the outdoor tables that cover much of the square in summer. The streets around Place Grenette are packed with shops, restaurants and bars.

Place aux Herbes

Around the Place aux Herbes are some of Grenoble's oldest houses, dating from the 16th and 17th centuries. The cobblestone area in the middle of the square is the site of a small marketplace. Restaurants and bars line the edges and surrounding streets, making this one of the liveliest spots in town.

Place Saint-André

This square in the heart of the Old Town is steeped in history. It is dominated by the grandest and formerly most important building in town, the Palais de Justice, which housed the Dauphiné Parliament. The centrepiece of the square is a statue of Bayard (aka Pierre Terrail), the legendary *chevalier sans peur et sans reproche* ('knight without fear and above reproach'), who was made lieutenant-general of Dauphiné in 1515.

Museums

Grenoble is a culture-rich city, catering to a wide range of interests with its themed and art museums.

Centre National d'Art Contemporain (CNAC, National Centre of Contemporary Art)

The cutting-edge National Centre is a major venue on the European art scene, despite its quiet location outside central Grenoble. This dynamic gallery constantly changes because there is no

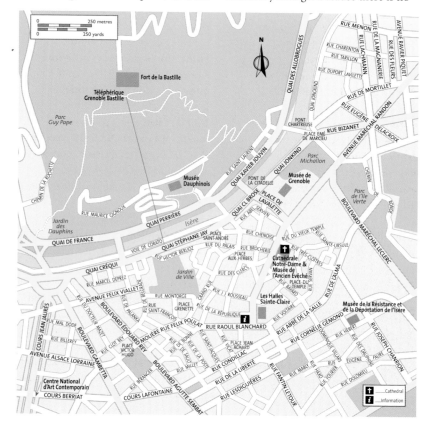

Grenoble and Isère

Leafy Boulevarde Gametta in central Grenoble

subjects relevant to Alpine life, from skiing to crafts and rural traditions, and there is a large collection of objects from archaeological sites.
30 rue Maurice Gignoux. Tel: (04) 76 85 19 01. www.musee-dauphinois.fr. Open: Jun–Sept 10am–7pm; Oct–May 10am–6pm. Closed: Tue. Free admission.

Musée de Grenoble (Grenoble Museum)

Grenoble's premier museum is also known as the Musée des Beaux-Arts (Museum of Fine Arts) and it has earned widespread recognition with its brilliant collections of 20th-century and classic paintings. The main museum building is contemporary but it also includes a medieval tower, the Tour de l'Îsle, where an impressive selection of drawings is displayed.
Place de Lavalette. Tel: (04) 76 63 44 44. www.museedegrenoble.fr (in French). Open: Wed–Mon 10am–6.30pm. Admission charge.

permanent collection. Based in a spacious warehouse called Le Magasin, the centre includes two huge, visually striking exhibition areas. Temporary exhibitions are planned directly with the individual artists, who design their works to fit the space or liaise with the gallery to adapt the space to the works.
155 cours Berriat, site Bouchayer-Viallet. Tel: (04) 76 21 95 84. www.magasin-cnac.org. Open: Tue–Sun 2–7pm. Admission charge (free for under 10s). Tram A: Berriat-Le Magasin.

Musée Dauphinois (Museum of Dauphiné)

Tucked away in an old convent building beneath the Fort de la Bastille is this charming museum dedicated to the cultural history of Dauphiné. Exhibitions explore a sweeping range of

Musée de la Résistance et de la Déportation de l'Isère (Isère Museum of Resistance and Deportation)

While the Nazis were deporting Jews and other persecuted groups from Grenoble to concentration camps, the Vercors region was a stronghold of the French Resistance. The museum remembers these local World War II events through emotive exhibitions, featuring photographs, posters, journals and film archives.

14 rue Hébert. Tel: (04) 76 42 38 53. www.resistance-en-isere.fr. Open: Sept–Jun Mon & Wed–Fri 9am–6pm, Tue 1.30–6pm, Sat & Sun 10am–7pm; Jul–Aug Wed–Mon 10am–7pm, Tue 1.30–7pm. Free admission.

Fort de la Bastille (Bastille Fort)

Perched on a hilltop above the river Isère, the fort is one of Grenoble's top attractions, offering an amazing panorama over the city and surrounding mountains, which are labelled by viewing tables at the lookout point. The first part of the fort dates from the 16th century, when a watchtower was built on the site, but most of the stronghold was constructed in the early 19th century to guard against potential attacks from Savoie.

There are three ways up this ascent of about 250m (820ft): by foot, by car or by cable car. Footpaths from the river are clearly signed and it takes approximately an hour to walk up the winding route. The route to and from the 'Porte de France' is the most leisurely, leading through a couple of parks – Parc Guy Pape and Jardin des Dauphins. There is an alternative path to and from the 'Porte Saint-Laurent' but this route includes a vertiginous 380-step stairway. It is also possible to start a longer hike into the Chartreuse from the top of the Bastille.
Free admission.

Téléphérique Grenoble Bastille (Grenoble Bastille Cable Car)

The cable car is a Grenoble icon and the sight of its cute bauble-like pods gliding over the river makes a great picture. It is a quick and entertaining way of getting to and from the fort, but

The cable car to Grenoble's Fort de la Bastille

queues build up at busy times of the year. Behind the cable-car station is the Jardin de Ville, a small town park useful for a picnic break.

Quai Stéphane Jay. Tel: (04) 76 44 33 65. Open: Feb–Nov. Admission charge.

Place Victor Hugo

In the stylish boutique shopping district, this is one of the most elegant locations in Grenoble. A vibrant Christmas market lights up the square every December, with classic wooden huts, carol singing and mulled wine contributing to the city's festive atmosphere.

Les Halles Sainte-Claire (St Clair Market)

Grenoble's largest market, based in a monumental hall built in 1874, supplies all the usual French market delights. An

Grenoble from the Fort du St Eynard

STENDHAL

Henri Beyle (1783–1842), who wrote under the pseudonym of Stendhal, became Grenoble's most famous son. Although he was writing at a time when French literature was all about Romanticism, Stendhal was one of the pioneers of Realism. His best-known works are the classic novels *Le Rouge et le Noir* ('The Red and the Black', 1830) and *La Chartreuse de Parme* ('The Charterhouse of Parma', 1839). He also penned several other novels and novellas (some unfinished), essays, biographies, memoirs and a non-fiction study about love (*De l'Amour*, 1822). Stendhal's early life in Grenoble is described in the posthumously published *Vie d'Henry Brulard* ('The Life of Henry Brulard'), an autobiographical story veiled as fiction.

additional open-air fruit and vegetable market is set up outside in the mornings.

Place Sainte-Claire. Open: Tue–Sun 7am–1pm, Fri–Sat 7am–1pm & 3–7pm.

Around Grenoble

The Maison de la Montagne in the city centre is an invaluable resource for planning activities in the area. Within the building are knowledgeable staff, a reference library and various local maps and walking guides for sale.

3 rue Raoul Blanchard. Tel: (04) 76 44 67 03. Open: Mon–Fri 9.30am–12.30pm & 1.30–6pm, Sat 10am–1pm & 2–5pm.

Château de Vizille

Twenty kilometres (12½ miles) south of Grenoble, the small town of Vizille is dominated by a regal castle set in vast landscaped grounds. Rebuilt in the 19th

century due to fire damage, the castle's style is that of the early 17th century, but its outline is slightly unbalanced. It now houses a museum dedicated to the French Revolution.
Tel: (04) 76 68 07 35/(04) 76 68 15 16. Open: Apr–Oct Wed–Mon 10am– 12.30pm & 1.30–6pm; Nov–Mar 10am– 12.30pm & 1.30–5pm. Free admission.

Chemin de Fer de La Mure (La Mure Mountain Railway)

This railway runs between the town of La Mure and the village of Saint-Georges-de-Commiers in the Drac valley. A seat on the historic little red train provides a unique perspective on the valley, traversing gorges across viaducts and chugging through tunnels. Opened in 1888, the line was at the cutting edge of railway engineering. La Mure was a coal-mining town until the 1990s and the railway was used to transport coal. In July and August, there are four departures per day in each direction. In May, June and September, there are two, and in October only one.
Tel: 0892 39 14 26. www.trainlamure.com. Open: May–Sept daily; Oct Wed, Sat & Sun. Tickets: €16.20 single, €19.20 return (concessions available). Reservations required.

Lacs de Laffrey

These four lakes – Lac Mort, Grand Lac de Laffrey, Lac de Petichet and Lac de Pierre-Châtel – form a chain alongside the N85 road just north of La Mure. A sailing and windsurfing school is based

Sailing on the Grand Lac de Laffrey

at the Grand Lac de Laffrey, which is an ideally sized lake for a gentle introduction to the sports. Swimming and fishing are possible here, too.

Sassenage

On the western outskirts of Grenoble, overlooked by the Vercors plateau, is the community of Sassenage. This leafy town has two main visitor attractions: a 17th-century castle and a set of ancient caves (*cuves*). The château and its landscaped gardens are open to the public. Guided tours of the caves allow access for an hour to an atmospheric underground land of natural stone sculptures and a waterfall.
Les Cuves de Sassenage. Tel: (04) 76 27 55 37. www.sassenage.fr. Guided tours: Apr, May & Oct Sat & Sun 1.30–4.30pm; Jun & Sept Tue–Sun 1.30–6pm; Jul & Aug daily 10am–6pm. Admission charge.

Feats of engineering

Transforming the Alps from a remote region, out of reach to all but the most adventurous or wealthy of visitors, to the popular destination of today required some incredible feats of engineering. Projects to make the mountains accessible started to take off in the 1890s and the early years of the 20th century, beginning with the introduction of railways to the Alps. Some of the first mountain railways to open connected Aix-les-Bains with Mont Revard (1892), Saint-Gervais-les-Bains with the Col de la Voza in the first stage of the Mont Blanc tramway (1909), and Chamonix with Montenvers and the Mer de Glace (1909).

Downhill skiing as a widely available leisure activity was made possible by a further engineering advancement: the development of cable cars. These had already been used around the world to transport objects – for example, in the mining industry – but the concept of using cables to transport people was still a novel one when two Swiss engineers first dreamt up the Aiguille du Midi cable car in 1905. Their plans proved too ambitious for the time and never reached fruition, but a French

company later took up the idea and successfully opened the first section of the route in 1924, adding an extension up to Les Glaciers in 1927. The cable car was rebuilt and extended in the early 1950s, finally reaching the Aiguille du Midi in 1955. Meanwhile, cable cars had begun to spring up across the French Alps. Grenoble's *téléphérique* to the Fort de la Bastille was opened in 1934, making it one of the first urban cable cars.

Mountain railways and cable cars connected resorts to the peaks above them, but linking up the mountains on a wider scale required a different type of engineering: the building of bridges. From 18th-century arched stone bridges to 20th-century concrete viaducts, the French Alps are full of fascinating solutions to the challenges of traversing rivers, gorges and valleys. Some of the most attractive examples include the viaduct over the Arve river at Les Houches and the bridges over the Gorges des Usses near Lac Léman.

As well as revolutionising transportation and tourism in the Alps, impressive engineering projects have been used to supply energy. The inspiration for the most significant development was the rivers gushing through the mountains. Hydroelectricity, now a major source of energy for the French Alps, was first introduced to the area in 1869 when an engineer called Aristide Bergès, working for a factory owner, harnessed a waterfall at Lancey, near Grenoble. As more and more waterfalls were put to work over the following decades, local industries received a boost of power that enabled them to develop. In the 1950s, the potential of hydroelectric power, or *houille blanche* ('white coal'), really took off as engineers became increasingly adventurous with their projects, building tunnels to channel water through the mountains and large reservoirs to hold it. Dams are now part of the Alpine architecture and many of them blend in surprisingly harmoniously with the landscape. The huge Tignes-Le Chevril dam, although a controversial project at first, has become a monument in its own right. There is even a museum dedicated to hydroelectricity, the **Musée Hydrelec** (*Le Verney, Vaujany. Tel: (04) 76 80 78 00. www.musee-hydrelec.fr. Open: mid-Jun–mid-Sept 10am–6pm; Sat & Sun, school holidays & mid-Sept–mid-Jun 2–6pm*).

Cable cars are the fastest way to reach the high summits

PARC NATUREL RÉGIONAL DU VERCORS

Stretching in a long line along the western side of Grenoble and south to the edge of the Isère region, the limestone cliffs of the Vercors make a dramatic impression when seen from the valley. Within the natural park the scenery is spectacular. Open plains give way to dense forests and deep river gorges. The high plateaux in the south of the park have extra protective status as a nature reserve (Réserve Naturelle des Hauts Plateaux). Golden eagles, eagle owls, chamois, ibexes, wild boar and wolves are among the wildlife found in the park. Driving through the Vercors is an experience in itself. Many

Pont-en-Royans' suspended houses (see p56)

A MOUNTAIN STRONGHOLD

With their unique strategic advantages and challenges, the Alps were fought over from the time of antiquity. During World War II, they saw a new batch of battles. *Maquis* (Resistance) fighters set up bases within the natural fortress of the Vercors, temporarily labelled the 'Forteresse de la Résistance'. The fiercest fights against German and Vichy forces took place in 1944 in the Vercors and at the Plateau des Glières in the Haute-Savoie. Losses were severe, but parts of the Alpine region were eventually liberated by Resistance efforts. Several memorials to the *maquis* fighters and local victims stand at significant sites, including the Forêt de Lente and the Route de Valchevrière near Villard-de-Lans.

of the roads have a cliff on one side and a river gorge on the other, and some, like Combe Laval and the Grands Goulets, go through tunnels and arches carved out of the rock. As well as dramatic cliff roads, the Vercors is also traversed by footpaths in summer and cross-country skiing trails in winter.

Grottes de Choranche (Choranche Caves)

Deep in the cliffs above the Gorges de la Bourne are these wonderful caves. They number seven in total, but only two are open to the public and only one, the Grotte de Coufin, can be explored without caving equipment. Guided tours introduce visitors to this incredible underground world of bizarre rock formations, stalactites and emerald lakes. There is also a nature trail outside the cave. Guided visits in English are available during July and August.

Tel: (04) 76 36 09 88.
*www.choranche.com. Open: Jul–Aug
10am–6.30pm; Apr–Jun & Sept–Oct
10am–noon & 1.30–5.30 or 6pm; Nov–
Feb Mon–Fri 1.30–4.30pm, Sat & Sun
10.30am–4.30pm; Mar Mon–Fri
11.30am–1.30pm & 1.30–4.30pm, Sat &
Sun 10.30am–4.30pm. Closed: 22
Nov–17 Dec. Admission charge.*

Villard-de-Lans

The principal winter centre of the
Vercors is mainly known for cross-
country skiing, but links to the slightly
higher resort of Corrençon-en-Vercors
open up a surprisingly sizeable and
varied area of downhill slopes. Other
snow-based pursuits in Villard-de-Lans
include sledging and snowshoeing. The
town is also equipped for summer
options such as walking, paragliding

and exploring the region's many caves.
Information about all these activities is
provided at the **Office de Tourisme**
(*Place Mure Ravaud. Tel: (04) 76 95 10
38. www.villarddelans.com*).

PARC NATUREL RÉGIONAL DE LA CHARTREUSE

Geographically, the Chartreuse is like a
smaller sibling to the Vercors. The
combination of limestone plateaux,
forests, gorges and caves is just as
stunning here as on the other side of
Grenoble, but on a more compact scale.
Culturally, the Chartreuse has a
distinctive heritage as the location of the
Grande Chartreuse monastery. Protected
as a natural regional park since 1995,
the area offers many beautiful
walking routes. The highest peaks –

(*Cont. on p58*)

Steep limestone cliffs are a trademark feature of the Vercors

Drive: Gorges and caves

This route takes in some of the most spectacular features of the Vercors landscape. Drive extremely cautiously, as the roads are very narrow in places, especially through the Grands Goulets. These winding roads are sometimes closed for maintenance work, so it is advisable to check at the tourist office in Villard-de-Lans before setting out.

The route covers 36km (22 miles) from Villard-de-Lans to Pont-en-Royans and 24km (15 miles) from Pont-en-Royans back to Villard-de-Lans. Allow a day to explore all the sites.

1 Villard-de-Lans

As the activity-planning centre of the Vercors, Villard-de-Lans makes a good starting point, with a tourist office to get information.

Take the main road, D531, out of town. After about 7km (4½ miles) the road crosses the Pont de la Goule Noire, a small bridge over the river bed.

2 Pont de la Goule Noire

The Goule Noire is a mountain spring that rises downstream of the bridge.

Turn left here on to the D103. Continue through the villages of Saint-Julien-en-Vercors and Saint-Martin-en-Vercors. At Les-Barraques-en-Vercors, turn right on to the D518 in the direction of Pont-en-Royans. This is the road through the Grands Goulets.

3 Grands Goulets

This deep river gorge traversed by a winding road clinging to the cliff is highly atmospheric. The road passes under overhanging rocks and through tunnels as it wends its way through.

Stay on the D518 as it meanders on to Pont-en-Royans (11km/7 miles).

4 Pont-en-Royans

Along the river is a row of *maisons suspendues* (literally 'suspended houses'), which are actually tall, thin houses attached to the cliff face. Built in the 15th and 16th centuries, they have stood the test of time remarkably well.

Take the D531 west and stay on this road to the junction with the D1532. Turn left for Saint-Nazaire.

5 Saint-Nazaire-en-Royans

This village has a picturesque waterfront location between the Isère river and an artificial lake fed by the Bourne river. By the lake is the Grotte Préhistorique de Thaïs.

6 La Sône

The village of La Sône can be visited by boat trip from Saint-Nazaire. At La Sône, there is an interesting park, the Jardin des Fontaines Pétrifiantes ('Garden of Petrifying Springs').

Retrace the route back to Pont-en-Royans and continue straight through on the D531. About 7km (4½ miles) after Pont-en-Royans you will reach a sign for the Grottes de Choranche. The caves are situated at the top of this small road, 3km (just under 2 miles) from the turn.

7 Grottes de Choranche

Guided visits of the most remarkable caves in the region take about an hour.

Return to the D531, turn left and continue towards Villard-de-Lans.

8 Gorges de la Bourne

The Bourne river gushes through a narrow gorge between steep cliff faces and the road follows its scenic course.

Take the D531 back to Villard-de-Lans.

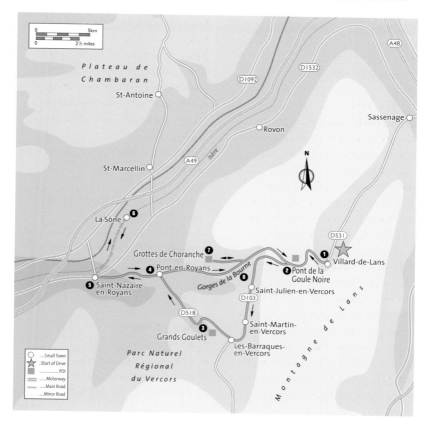

The pretty Chartreuse countryside

Chamechaude, Grand Som and Dent de Crolles – just exceed 2,000m (6,560ft).

Chartreuse cellars

At the Chartreuse cellars visitors can learn about how the curious dark green liqueur is produced and take a tour of the cellar with a tasting included.
10 boulevard Edgar-Koffler, Voiron. Tel: (04) 76 05 81 77. www.chartreuse.fr. Open: Apr–May & Sept–Oct 9–11.30am & 2–6.30pm; Jul–Aug 9am–6.30pm; Nov–Dec & Feb–Mar Mon–Fri 9–11.30am & 2–5.30pm. Free admission.

Château de Touvet

Through a combination of preservation and remodelling, the Château de Touvet stands complete in the same hilltop spot above the Grésivaudan valley where a medieval fort was built in the 13th century. The round towers with pointed roofs formed part of the original structure, but most of the castle has a 15th-century exterior with 18th-century interiors and landscaped gardens. Although the castle is still inhabited, it is open to the public in the summer months.

THE ELIXIR OF LIFE

The Carthusian monks of the Chartreuse started producing their famous liqueur, poetically described as 'the elixir of life', in the 16th century. The secret formula for the liqueur survived several destructions and persecutions of the monastery and was passed down through the generations. Today, it is produced in the Chartreuse cellars in Voiron (*see above*). Distilled from wine, honey and the essence of 130 different plants, the elixir of life packs a powerful punch at 71 per cent proof. As well as the classic Chartreuse, the monks also developed several other liqueurs, including Génépi (from Alpine flowers), walnut and fruit varieties.

*Tel: (04) 76 08 42 27. www.touvet.com.
Open: Jul–Aug Sun–Fri 2–6pm; Apr–Jun
& Sept–Oct Sun & public holidays
2–6pm. Admission charge.*

Fort du Saint-Eynard

Perched on a cliff at the edge of the
Chartreuse massif, this fort boasts an
unrivalled view of Grenoble, the valley
and the peaks of Belledonne, Oisans,
Trièves and Vercors. A viewing table
labels the visible mountains. Guided
visits around the fort take place on
Sunday afternoons at 2.30 and 3.30pm.
There is also a restaurant, open from
May to October except on Sunday
evenings and Mondays.
*Tel: (04) 76 85 25 24. Open: May–Jun &
Sept–Oct Thur–Sun noon–11pm;
Jul–Aug Wed–Sun noon–11pm.
Free admission.*

Saint-Pierre-de-Chartreuse

Situated on the eastern margin of the
natural park beneath wooded hills and
limestone cliffs, this amiable village is a
good base for walking and mountain
biking. In winter, there is access to a
small area of downhill skiing on Scia
mountain, as well as cross-country ski
trails and snowshoe walking circuits.
The nearby Monastère de la Grande
Chartreuse has been home to monks of
the Saint-Bruno order since 1084. Due
to the silent lifestyle of the monks, the
monastery is not open to visitors, but
the **Musée de la Grande Chartreuse**
tells its story (*La Correrie. Tel: (04) 76
88 60 45. www.musee-grande-
chartreuse.fr. Open: May–Sept 10am–
6.30pm; Apr & Oct–Nov Mon–Fri
1.30–6pm, Sat & Sun 10am–6pm.
Admission charge*).

The Fort du Saint-Eynard overlooking the Grésivaudan valley and Châine de Belledonne

Tour: Chartreuse

Traversing the Chartreuse from south to north, this tour features views of some of the most outstanding scenery in the park.

The drive from Grenoble to the Col du Granier is about 75km (46 miles), the total round trip is about 145km (90 miles).

Start at the Musée de Grenoble. Drive across the river on the Pont de la Citadelle and turn right, following road signs for the Chartreuse to get on to the D512.

The Fort du Saint-Eynard is signposted on a right turn from the D512.

1 Fort du Saint-Eynard

Unrivalled views over Grenoble and the surrounding mountains at the fort.
Return to the D512 and head north. Continue uphill on the D512 to the Col de Porte pass.

2 Col de Porte

There are a couple of detour options. A left turn takes you up to Charmant Som for a viewpoint over the Chartreuse monastery.
Continue along the D512 towards Saint-Pierre-de-Chartreuse and turn left on to the D520B, signposted to Saint-Laurent-du-Pont. After 2.5km (1½ miles), take the small right turn to the museum at La Correrie, 1.5km (1 mile) from the turn.

3 Musée de la Grande Chartreuse

Learn about the Carthusian monks whose fascinating history is famously linked with the area at this museum set in 17th–18th-century monastic buildings.
Return to the D512 junction and turn left for Saint-Pierre-de-Chartreuse.

4 Saint-Pierre-de-Chartreuse

As one of the main villages in the Chartreuse, this makes a good stop-off point for information and a lunch or coffee break.
Continue north on the D512, in the direction of Saint-Pierre-d'Entremont. A couple of kilometres out of the village there is a right turn to La Scia. You can drive up this road (it turns into a bumpy dirt track). Or take the next right turn from the D512 to the bottom of the Combe de l'Ours chairlift, where you can park and purchase a ticket.

5 La Scia

From the car park or top of the chairlift, scramble up a little path for a more panoramic view.
Return to the D512 and continue north. At the village of Saint-Pierre-

d'Entremont, take a right turn on to the D45C to the Cirque de Saint-Même chalet. The natural site is about a 30-minute walk from the car park. Note that there is a charge of €3 for parking.

6 Cirque de Saint-Même

The 'circus' consists of waterfalls gushing down a limestone cliff.
Return to Saint-Pierre-d'Entremont and turn right on to the D912 towards Chambéry. After passing through

Entremont-le-Vieux, the road begins to climb to the Col du Granier pass.

7 Col du Granier

Mont Granier (1,933m/6,340ft) is one of the most distinctive Chartreuse landmarks. From the pass, there are several marked walking trails in the hills facing the mountain, which are suitable for easy strolls.
Continue down the D912 to Chambéry and take the fast route A41 back to Grenoble.

Tour: Chartreuse

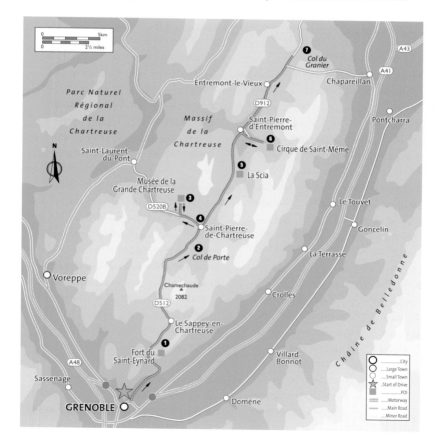

The glacial summits of the Écrins from Col du Glaibier

LES ÉCRINS AND OISANS

The loftiest peaks in Isère are clustered in the southeast corner of the region around the town of Le Bourg d'Oisans. This rugged glacial landscape has its fair share of Alpine contrasts, with busy mountain resorts located just a short distance from the margins of the rugged Écrins national park. Details of the park, which straddles the border between Isère and Hautes-Alpes, are covered in the 'Southern Alps' chapter (*see p118*).

L'Alpe d'Huez

L'Alpe d'Huez is a large winter sports resort at 1,860m (6,100ft), which transforms into a popular cycling, hiking and mountaineering destination in the summer. Inhabited since antiquity, the Huez area has a long history of silver and coal mining. Having welcomed tourists since the 1920s, L'Alpe d'Huez is also one of the longest-established ski resorts around. The centre developed in a piecemeal fashion over the decades and is hardly beautiful, but hop on one of the lifts into the Massif des Grandes Rousses and there is plenty of picturesque scenery to compensate. With a high point of 3,330m (10,925ft), the ski area affords amazing views over a large swathe of the Alps. One of the best panoramas is from the Pic Blanc, which can be reached in summer as well as winter via cable cars.

In total, there are 245km (152 miles) of pistes, a huge extent for a single resort, and the variety is fantastic. The slopes range from a large web of novice-suited greens near the resort to the record-setting 16km (10-mile) La Sarenne, the longest piste in the Alps, which is classified black. A weekly lift pass covers an optional day in Les Deux Alpes or Serre-Chevalier, as well as lots of the resort facilities, including swimming pools, an ice rink and a sports centre. **The Office de Tourisme** (*Tel: (04) 76 11 44 44. www.alpedhuez.com. Open: high season 9am–7pm; low season Mon–Fri 9am–12.30pm & 2.30–6pm*) is located in the Maison de l'Alpe on Place Paganon and sells lift passes.

In summer, keen cyclists flock to L'Alpe d'Huez to challenge themselves with the legendary ride up from Le Bourg d'Oisans, a popular Tour de France stage. Cyclists not up for the punishing climb can arrive in the resort by other means and enjoy a network of mountain-bike trails accessed via the lifts.

Les Deux Alpes

Convenience (there is a bus service from Grenoble), relative affordability, a lively vibe and the chance to ski or snowboard at dizzying heights all contribute to the popularity of this resort. From the resort at 1,600m (5,250ft), it is a long way up to the Glacier du Mont de Lans (3,200m–3,425m/10,500ft–11,235ft) at the top of the ski area, which even offers summer skiing. The views from the glacier are simply spectacular and, unusually for such high-altitude skiing, the slopes are fairly easy. Further down the mountain, skiers and boarders can choose from several sections of pistes and a renowned snow park.

In the resort there is plenty to keep visitors occupied off the slopes, both during the day and at night. Alternative daytime options include swimming in a heated pool, ice-skating and snowmobile expeditions. For something less active, try a visit to the Grotte de Glace (*Open: 10am–3pm. Admission charge*), an ice cave which is accessible by cable car. When the lifts

High in the mountains above L'Alpe d'Huez

stop running, the après-ski scene gets going, with a good choice of bars and restaurants.

The resort's main drawback is the crowds. At peak times, lift queues tend to build up and the slopes back to the village get unpleasantly congested at the end of the day. In summer, Les Deux Alpes is less busy, but still popular. Various guided expeditions, such as canyoning and rock climbing, are on offer and there are trails for hiking and mountain biking. For general information, visit the Maison des Deux Alpes on Place des Deux Alpes, home to the **Office de Tourisme** (*Tel: (04) 76 79 22 00*) plus accommodation and guiding services.

Les Deux Alpes is linked to nearby expert-skiers' paradise La Grave (see p118).

Les Deux Alpes resort

PISTE CLASSIFICATIONS AND LIFTS

French resorts use a four-level difficulty classification system. Green pistes are very easy and suitable for beginners progressing from the short nursery slopes to longer runs. Blue pistes are fairly easy and generally perfect for leisurely cruising, but with some slightly steeper, bumpier or narrower sections. Reds are more difficult and suited to advancing intermediates. Finally, black runs present the ultimate on-piste challenge. Different types of mechanical lifts take skiers and snowboarders up the slopes, including chairlifts, drag lifts, cable cars, gondolas and funicular railways. With the exception of drag lifts, lifts run in both directions, providing an alternative to skiing back down. They generally stay open until about 4 or 5pm.

Le Bourg d'Oisans

As the main town in the area, Le Bourg d'Oisans is a good place to get information about the Parc National des Écrins. The **Maison du Parc** (*Rue Gambetta. Tel: (04) 76 80 00 51. Open: Jul–Aug 9am–7pm; Sept–Jun Mon–Fri 9–11am & 2–5pm*) and the **Office de Tourisme** (*Quai Girard. Tel: (04) 76 80 03 25. www. bourgdoisans.com*) are both useful sources. Buses link the town to L'Alpe d'Huez and Les Deux Alpes ski resorts (both just 40 minutes away), as well as Grenoble and Briançon. The twisting and turning route up to L'Alpe d'Huez, which includes 21 hairpin bends in 14km (8½ miles), is one of the major Alpine challenges of the Tour de France.

CHAINE DE BELLEDONNE

Belledonne, which rises in a chain of peaks above the Isère valley on the eastern side, is the closest high-altitude range to Grenoble. It includes the Massif de Chamrousse, the Massif d'Allevard and several high valleys and small- to medium-sized mountain resorts.

Chamrousse

At just 35km (22 miles) from Grenoble and accessible by bus, the compact ski resort of Chamrousse is convenient for day-trippers. It is an ideal place to sample the sport for beginners unsure about launching into a full-scale ski holiday, as much of the ski terrain is gentle. Experienced skiers can have fun here too though, especially on the Olympic black runs. With a resort height of 1,650m (5,415ft) and maximum elevation of 2,255m

(7,400ft), the slopes are appealingly tree-lined. Summer activities are also available and there is a great view from the Croix de Chamrousse, accessible by cable car in July and August. For information on summer and winter activities, visit the **Office de Tourisme** on Place de Belledonne (*Tel: (04) 76 89 92 65. www.chamrousse.com*).

Les Sept Laux

Sept Laux is another family-friendly, fairly small resort within easy reach of Grenoble, located in the Vallée du Haut Bréda in the heart of the Chaîne de Belledonne. Facilities are divided between three villages: Prapoutel, Pipay and Pleynet. The variation in altitude is 1,350m (4,430ft) to 2,400m (7,875ft) and much of the terrain is pretty and forested. In summer, it is possible to hike to the seven glacier lakes above the resort.

Grenoble and Isère

The Chaîne de Belledonne mountain range from Grenoble's Fort de la Bastille

Savoie

Savoie is the ultimate skiing destination, an adrenalin-seeker's paradise of vast linked resorts and plentiful snow. It is also dramatically beautiful, from glacial heights to pine-forested slopes to the shores of Lac du Bourget. Surveying the landscape from one of the many panoramic viewpoints, no stretch of the imagination is needed to see why this region was so fiercely contested for so long.

Savoie's history is most evident in the area around Chambéry, the original capital of the duchy and the location of the Château des Ducs de Savoie. Testaments to earlier history can be found at nearby Aix-les-Bains, where some Roman ruins remain. Aix is, however, better known as a spa town and base for watersports on the picturesque Lac du Bourget. Throughout the region, Savoie's unique cultural heritage is evident in arts and crafts, place names, festivals and, of course, the hearty food.

However, the majority of visitors to Savoie come for the excellent downhill skiing and snowboarding opportunities, undoubtedly some of the best in the world. Within the majestic heights of the Massif de la Vanoise are three extensive ski areas: Les Trois Vallées, Espace Killy and Paradiski. Their combined statistics are impressive: eight major well-equipped resorts and a handful of smaller satellites; over 1,300km (805 miles) of groomed pistes; more than 400 lifts; and high slopes extending up to altitudes of 3,000m (9,840ft) plus.

In summer, many of Savoie's resorts welcome other sports enthusiasts, with hiking, rock climbing, paragliding and mountain biking among the activities on offer. The rugged Parc National de la Vanoise (*see p75*) also draws visitors to its scenic nature trails and lovely mountain villages.

Les Trois Vallées

Practically unrivalled for extent and variety, this ski area includes around 600km (375 miles) of pistes and some 200 lifts to link them all. The three valleys in question are, from west to east, Courchevel (Saint-Bon), Méribel (Allues) and Belleville, which includes Val Thorens, Les Menuires and Saint-Martin-de-Belleville. A fourth valley, the Maurienne, is also linked up via Orelle. Bargain alternatives for visitors who do not mind a longer lift ride in the

(*Cont. on p70*)

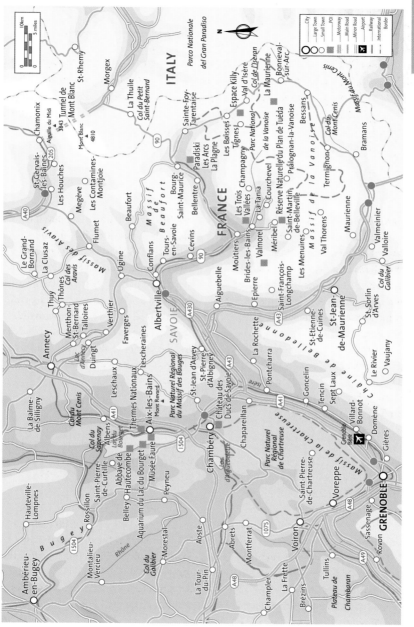

Choosing a winter sports resort

There are so many winter sports resorts in the French Alps that deciding where to go can present a significant challenge. Variables can be broadly grouped into two categories: the resort (price, facilities, activities, style of accommodation, nightlife, size, convenience and ambience) and the slopes (altitude, scenery, extent and difficulty).

Families

The Portes du Soleil resorts of Avoriaz and Les Gets offer excellent children's facilities and activities, as does Flaine. Nearer Grenoble, Chamrousse is very family-friendly. The small, family-oriented linked resorts of Valmorel and Saint-François-Longchamp are ideal places for children to learn as their mainly easy and middling pistes do not appeal to speed fiends.

Mixed-ability groups

Many ski resorts have pistes suitable for all abilities, but mixed-ability groups can sometimes end up having to split up and ski in different sectors. Les Arcs avoids this issue because from most of the lifts there is a choice of varied-level pistes. Méribel also has well-balanced sectors and its position at the centre of Les Trois Vallées makes it ideal for keeping everyone happy.

Beginners

Les Arcs offers lessons using a revolutionary *ski évolutif* technique, where you start on short skis and progress to the normal length. Resorts with nearby interesting towns (such as Serre-Chevalier) or lots of alternative activities (such as Alpe d'Huez) are also good choices.

Experts

Chamonix and La Grave both offer celebrated and very challenging off-piste terrain – Chamonix on the slopes of Mont Blanc and La Grave in the Écrins. Tignes has lots of off-piste accessible from lifts. L'Alpe d'Huez is good for all abilities, but has a couple of perks for the adventurous: a black run (La Sarenne), which is the longest piste in the Alps, and certificates for anyone who skis 8,000m (26,245ft) of elevation in one day.

Snowboarders

Snow parks are widespread, but the one at Les Deux Alpes is renowned. The Espace Killy is also very popular with boarders.

Après-ski
Resorts with a particularly dynamic nightlife include Morzine, Val d'Isère, Chamonix and Méribel.

Affordability
Les Deux Alpes, Flaine and Les Menuires are all large resorts with a good choice of relatively cheap self-catering accommodation and extensive skiing.

Mountain scenery
Snowy mountains will always look beautiful, but some resorts are particularly blessed in the scenery department. Courchevel and Montgenèvre are among the prettiest.

Authentic villages
Megève, Samoëns and La Clusaz are all lovely traditional villages that have welcomed the arrival of winter sports without losing their authentic characters. Another good bet is to choose a quiet village linked to a big ski area like Vaujany (L'Alpe d'Huez), Saint-Martin-de-Belleville (Les Trois Vallées) or Champagny (La Plagne).

Day trips
Visitors staying in Grenoble have a choice of local ski resorts. Chamrousse and Villard-de-Lans are both served by buses from the city and the VFD Skiligne deal offers a discount on return tickets and day ski passes bought together. La Clusaz can easily be visited on day trips from Annecy.

Long season
Val Thorens is the highest resort at 2,300m (7,545ft), and at 2,100m (6,890ft) Tignes is not far below. Both are very snow sure and have winter seasons that extend into late spring.

Off the radar
The French Alps contain numerous small but interesting resorts that receive limited international attention.
Examples are Auron, Valloire-Valmeinier, Sainte-Foy-Tarentaise, Pralognan-la-Vanoise and Villard-de-Lans. Brush up on your French before going!

A snowboarder is pulled up a drag lift in L'Alpe d'Huez

Wooden chalets in Courchevel

mornings are provided by the small spa town of Brides-les-Bains (connected to Méribel by a cable car) and purpose-built La Tania, which is linked to Courchevel. Adult winter lift passes for the whole area cost €46.50 for one day or €232 for six. In summer, when a scaled-down lift network operates, adult passes are €15 for a day or €42 for a week. Les Trois Vallées, like the rest of the Vanoise, is not easily accessible without a car, although nearby Moûtiers functions as a public transport hub.

Courchevel

Stylish Courchevel is one of the biggest names in Alpine skiing. Established in 1945, it was one of the earliest purpose-built ski resorts and it has remained a trendsetter ever since. Courchevel has four separate villages named after their altitudes (1850, 1650, 1550 and 1300) and a vast range of picturesque and varied slopes satisfying skiers and

boarders of all abilities. The downside is that this is one of the most expensive resorts in the Alps. Top-end hotels, gastronomic restaurants, luxury chalets and super-chic bars turn up the glitz factor, especially in the hugely popular 1850 village. However, there are also reasonably priced options to be found. When the snow melts, Courchevel turns into a surprisingly restful summer resort, providing access to some beautiful walking routes and a good range of activities. There are **Offices de Tourisme** in each of the villages (*www.courchevel.com*), with the main one located at 1850 (*Tel: (04) 79 08 00 29. Open: Jul–Aug & Dec–Apr 9am–7pm; Sept–Nov & May–Jun Mon–Fri 9am–noon & 2–6pm*).

Les Menuires

Les Menuires offers a cheaper alternative to Courchevel or Méribel. Although not as attractive or glamorous as its neighbours, it is equally well located for exploring Les Trois Vallées, with particularly quick links to Val Thorens. The centre of the resort is around the La Croisette lift, where there is a cluster of shops and services, including the **Office de Tourisme** (*Tel: (04) 79 00 73 00. www.lesmenuires.com*). Unfortunately, this is also where the most unattractive buildings are located, but all the slope-side accommodation does increase convenience and Les Menuires is gradually improving its image by adding stylish new chalet-style buildings.

Méribel

With a great variety of local slopes, a long history and entirely chalet-style architecture, Méribel gives Courchevel a run for its money. Its location in the central valley makes it a great headquarters for experiencing as much of the area as possible. Since its creation by a Scotsman in 1938, Méribel has remained hugely popular with British visitors. The resort consists of two main villages – Méribel and Méribel-Mottaret – both of which have sprawled to meet demand. In summer, hiking in the Parc National de la Vanoise is

possible, as some of the Méribel valley is included within this conservation area. Among the superb walking routes is a trail through the **Réserve Naturelle du Plan de Tuéda** (*Maison de la Réserve, Lac de Tuéda. Tel: (04) 79 01 04 75. www.vanoise.com. Open: Jul–Aug 12.30–6pm*). This reserve protects an ancient forest of arolla pines, an endangered Alpine species. Méribel's **Office de Tourisme** has further information (*Tel: (04) 79 08 60 01. www.meribel.net*).

Saint-Martin-de-Belleville

As a late addition to the Les Trois Vallées collection, the lovely old village of Saint-Martin has been only gently developed and has retained a peaceful ambience. Saint-Martin is ideal for visitors seeking a significantly quieter, less expensive Three Valleys trip. The slopes around the village are best for intermediates and not as consistently snow sure as higher areas, but chairlift links to Les Menuires and Méribel open up other possibilities. Village facilities include a few shops, restaurants and bars, a pretty old church and an **Office**

Méribel valley

de Tourisme (*Tel: (04) 79 00 20 00.*
www.st-martin-belleville.com).

Val Thorens

Sitting at the top of the Belleville valley, Val Thorens (2,300m/7,545ft) is the highest Alpine resort. The altitude guarantees a long, delightfully snowy season, but it also means that the treeless slopes are exposed to bad weather conditions. On sunny days, the skiing and snowboarding here are excellent for all levels of ability, offering everything from good nursery slopes to long, wonderfully varied runs. One of the most spectacular views is from the 3,195m (10,480ft) Cîme de Caron. Down at resort level, plenty of shops, restaurants and services, plus a large sports centre, are fitted into the compactly designed village. The après-

AVALANCHE BULLETINS

Avalanches are one of the main threats of the mountains and it is vital to check bulletins before venturing on to off-piste snow. Some avalanches occur naturally after heavy snowfalls, while others are triggered by people, particularly off-piste skiers and snowboarders. Méteo France produces a daily snow and avalanche bulletin throughout the winter, which is posted in mountain resorts. The resorts also highlight levels of risk in each area of slopes through an attention-grabbing system of flags: yellow for 'low risk', chequered yellow and black for 'heightened risk' and black for 'severe risk'. You can check the avalanche forecast online at *www.meteo.fr* or in English at *www.henrysavalanchetalk.com*

ski scene is fairly lively. As part of a traffic-minimisation scheme, visitors are allowed to drive into the village only to offload luggage. Shuttle buses are provided from peripheral car parks.

The vast Espace Killy ski area from the Grande Motte glacier

The Lac de Chevril near Tignes

The **Office de Tourisme** (*Maison de Val Thorens. Tel: (04) 79 00 08 08. www.valthorens.com*) provides parking details as well as general information. In summer, the high mountain scenery is more dramatic than pretty and attracts mainly mountaineers.

Espace Killy

Located in the dramatically beautiful upper Tarentaise valley on the northeastern edge of the Vanoise, the high-altitude Espace Killy ski area is internationally renowned. It connects Tignes and Val d'Isère, two very different and complementary centres. With 300km (185 miles) of pistes and a long snow season (late November to early May), this is a supreme winter sports destination. For visitors looking to cover even more ski miles, a six-day lift pass (€218) includes an optional day in Les Trois Vallées (*see p66*),

Paradiski (*see p75*) or Valmorel (*see p77*). One-day adult winter passes cost €44.50. The proximity of the Vanoise National Park and the availability of a full range of activities also attract summer visitors. Between Val d'Isère and Tignes is one of the most striking examples of Alpine hydroelectricity projects: the Lac du Chevril dam and reservoir lake, built in the 1950s.

Tignes

Purpose-built Tignes is a large modern resort which is lively in winter and summer and has a broad appeal. It is family-friendly and also attracts a lot of young groups. A cheerful ambience helps make up for the lack of architectural charm in the resort buildings. The resort consists of two main centres – Tignes-le-Lac and Val Claret – as well as the smaller Tignes-les-Boisses and Tignes-les-Brevières. At

2,100m (6,890ft), Tignes is high enough to be blanketed in snow for a big chunk of the year and the interesting slopes will delight intermediate and advanced skiers and snowboarders. There are a few very good nursery slopes in Tignes-le-Lac, although conveniently located, long, easy pistes are a bit lacking. In summer, the boating lake and surrounding area are the life and soul of the resort. The **Office de Tourisme** (*Tel: (04) 79 40 04 40. www.tignes.net*) advises on myriad activities.

Val d'Isère

Val d'Isère is a traditional high-mountain village which is transformed into an upmarket, high-adrenalin winter resort when the snow falls. Fantastic skiing and a buzzing nightlife have contributed to Val's international popularity, as has the prettiness of the

HIGH MOUNTAIN PASSES

Getting across the mountains from one rural valley to the next necessitates going over *cols* (passes) near the summits. The roads climbing up to and winding down from these tend to be dramatically beautiful, but also challenging to drive. Hairpin bends and narrow sections are a standard feature, as are dangerous drivers. At the top there is usually a *table d'orientation* (viewing table), labelling the visible mountains, and a restaurant, sometimes with a shop. From north to south, some of the most scenic passes are: Col des Aravis, Col du Petit Saint-Bernard (across the French–Italian border), Col de l'Iseran, Col du Mont Cenis, Col du Galibier and Col de la Bonette.

village. Much of the accommodation is in classic chalets or stylish hotels and there is a pedestrian centre with boutique shops, all of which ensures that charm is as thick on the ground as snow. Unsurprisingly, winter stays do not come cheap. The skiing is brilliant for intermediates and experts, but not

Val d'Isère seen from La Solaise

for progressing beginners – some of the pistes classified as greens are reportedly more like blues. In summer, Val d'Isère is quieter, with a down-to-earth feel, although it still offers plenty of activities. The Bellevarde cable car and Solaise chairlift operate for walkers and mountain bikers and there are trails back down to the resort. From the top of the Solaise there is an incredible view over the resort and the Lac du Chevril. Val d'Isère also serves as a gateway to the Vanoise National Park. **The Office de Tourisme** (*Place Jacques Mouflier. Tel: (04) 79 06 06 60. www.valdisere. com*) can advise on excursions.

Parc National de la Vanoise

Parc National de la Vanoise

Created in 1963 to preserve the fragile ecosystem of the upper Tarentaise and Maurienne valleys and the high mountains of the Vanoise massif, this is the oldest French national park. In the core zone, a layer of wildlife-rich forests fades into numerous glacier-capped, 3,000m (9,840ft) plus summits. Summer hikers can explore this beautiful scenery, keeping an eye out for the many animals that make it their home. Even if the ibexes, chamois, golden eagles, black grouses, owls and others stay out of sight, there are 1,000 different plant species to admire. The peripheral area of the park, not being subject to such stringent conservation rules, is traversed by winding roads and ski pistes as well as more walking paths. There are also some very pretty mountain villages, such as Bonneval-sur-Arc, where the **Office de Tourisme** (*Tel: (04) 79 05 95 95*) gives out park information.

Paradiski

On a bright winter day, riding a chairlift over pine trees and glittering snow drifts, the ambitious name of this large ski area actually seems quite apt. Even by Alpine standards, the views here are magnificent. Paradiski includes the major resorts of Les Arcs and La Plagne (linked by the huge double-decker Vanoise Express cable car), as well as the smaller centre of Peisey-Vallandry. The nearest town is Bourg-Saint-Maurice (*see p77*), which has a funicular railway to Arc 1600. There is an **information centre** by the funicular (*Place de la Gare. Tel: (04) 79 41 55 55. www.lesarcs.com*). Adult winter lift passes cost €48 for one day and €249 for six.

Les Arcs

Facilities at Les Arcs are divided across four resort villages (1600, 1800, 1950 and 2000), linked by road and by snow. Quiet Arc 1600 is a welcoming family-oriented place. Although small, it has a decent selection of shops and restaurants. Arc 1800 is the biggest of the villages, with a bit more going on. Arc 2000 is fairly uninteresting, although it enables quick access to the high slopes. Finally, Arc 1950 is the new kid on the block, built fairly recently and in a more attractive style that combines traditional wood buildings with colourful modern details. It has a good choice of places to stay and to eat, shops and evening entertainments. Les Arcs is one of the few resorts with enough varied terrain to keep

Sunset in Les Arcs

ski novices, intermediates and experts alike happy. The convenient link to neighbouring La Plagne also helps. In summer, with several lifts running, the network of mountain-biking trails is one of the best in the Alps. One of the most accessible places for summer pedestrians to enjoy a fantastic view is L'Arpette, near the top of the La Cachette chairlift from 1600. The highest point of the resort is Aiguille Rouge (3,226m/10,584ft), reachable by cable car in summer and winter, weather conditions permitting.

La Plagne

La Plagne has ten self-contained resort villages, making it one of the most spread-out ski centres in the French Alps. In the main central area, distinctively shaped like a large bowl, are Plagne-Centre, Plagne 1800, Plagne-Soleil, Aime, Belle-Plagne and Bellecôte. Free buses link these resorts during the day and in the evening. Montchavin, Les Coches, Montalbert and Champagny are further out and lower down. They are quieter and generally prettier than the central bowl's purpose-built villages, but less convenient for access to the whole Paradiski zone. The **Office de Tourisme** (*Tel: (04) 79 09 79 79. www.la-plagne.com*) can help visitors navigate the complex layout. La Plagne is fantastic for intermediates, but also caters well to other abilities. For something different, try the Olympic bobsleigh run.

Looking towards Mont Blanc from Roche de Mio in La Plagne

Bourg-Saint-Maurice

This quiet valley town is surrounded by high mountains and serves as a gateway to several of Savoie's main ski areas. Paradiski is closest and wonderfully easy to reach, thanks to the funicular railway between Bourg train station and the resort of Arc 1600. With the train taking just seven minutes to make the ascent, staying in this town is a viable alternative. Evening entertainment options are fairly limited, but there are several cosy restaurants serving up traditional Savoyard dishes. Long-distance TGV (high-speed) trains also stop here, linking the Alps to the UK via Eurostar.

Valmorel

Although Valmorel is a modern ski resort (built in 1975), it has the feel of a classic village. It forms part of a linked ski area with the smaller resorts of Saint-François-Longchamp, Celliers and Doucy-Combelouvière, collectively called Le Grand Domaine (adult lift passes €36.50 one-day, €186 six-day).

Lac du Bourget

Covering an area of over 4,400 hectares (17sq miles), the Lac du Bourget is France's biggest natural lake. Boat cruises and numerous watersports are available, including sailing, windsurfing and waterskiing. Aix-les-Bains is the main town, but there are several smaller centres around the shores. It is possible to drive a circuit around the lake, enjoying fantastic views as the route twists, climbs and descends. Picturesque points include the Col du Sapenay, overlooking the northern shore, Baie de Grésine, north of Aix, and the Chapelle Notre-Dame de l'Étoile, across from Aix.

Abbaye de Hautecombe

Benedictine monks first settled on the shore of Lac du Bourget in the early 12th century, and by the 14th century their quiet abbey retreat had prospered into one of the most important sites in Savoie. Although the abbey subsequently fell into decline for several hundred years, it was restored to its former glory during the 19th century. The abbey houses the tombs of many royals of the House of Savoie, including the last king and queen of Italy, all ornamented with marble and stone statues.
Saint-Pierre-de-Curtille. Tel: (04) 79 54 26 12. Open: mid-Feb–late Dec Wed–Mon 10–11.15am & 2–5pm; late Dec–mid-Feb Wed–Mon 2.30–5pm. Admission charge (free for under 18s).

Aix-les-Bains

Historic Aix-les-Bains, known for its hot springs since Roman times, is a pleasant spa town centred on the Thermes Nationaux (National Baths, *see below*). Traces of old-fashioned grandeur resonate from the palatial hotels near the baths, but the overall impression is of a lively modern town, particularly around the park, open-air theatre and shopping streets. On the shore of Lac du Bourget there are several beaches, a marina and a lovely promenade. Just outside town, the privately run Aix-Marlioz baths have

offered medicinal hydrotherapy since 1861.

Aquarium du Lac du Bourget

This large freshwater aquarium highlights the diversity of fish supported by the Lac du Bourget and other rivers and lakes.
Le Petit Port. Tel: (04) 79 61 08 22. www.aquarium-lacdubourget.com. Open: May–Sept 10am–7pm; Feb–Apr & Oct–Nov 2–6pm. Admission charge.

Musée Faure

This art museum is one of Aix's top attractions. It houses an impressive collection of artworks that were gifted to the town by Dr Faure in 1942.
Tel: (04) 79 61 06 57. Open: Wed–Mon 10am–noon & 1.30–6pm. Admission charge.

Thermes Nationaux

The Thermes Nationaux form a one-stop tour of the history of bathing in Aix. In 1783, Victor-Amadeus III of Savoie founded the Établissement Royal des Bains (Royal Baths) building around the few remaining structures of the old Roman baths. Following extensions in the 19th century to meet growing demand, the 1930s and 1970s brought further enhancement and modernisation, all resulting in an architectural melting pot which includes an Art Deco entrance hall, monumental 18th-century staircase and some original Roman marble. It is also possible, through a tunnel from the baths, to visit

the atmospheric hillside caves where the hot springs have their source.
Tel: (04) 79 35 38 50. Open: May–Oct. Admission charge.

La Maurienne

La Maurienne is the valley of the river Arc, running between the Massif de la Vanoise and the Massif du Mont Cenis in the southeastern corner of Savoie. The most dramatically scenic section is in the upper reaches between the Col de l'Iseran and the Col du Mont Cenis. Industrialisation further down has sadly detracted from the valley's natural beauty.

A traditional stone house in Bonneval-sur-Arc

Bonneval-sur-Arc

Charming Bonneval is a traditional stone village in the upper Maurienne on the edge of the Parc National de la Vanoise. Cars are not allowed in the tranquil village centre. There are several speciality shops selling local produce, including cheeses, meats and bread, and gifts such as pottery and woodwork. In winter, there is access to a small but usually very snowy ski area, while summer activities include hiking and mountaineering. The **Office de Tourisme** (*Tel: (04) 79 05 95 95*) provides information and maps.

Valloire-Valmeinier

The linked village-resorts of Valloire and Valmeinier make up the main ski area of the Maurienne, offering downhill and cross-country skiing. At the heart of Valloire village is an attractive 17th-century Baroque church. Local lore tells that the residents clubbed together to contribute the building materials, creating one of the most ornamented churches in Savoie.

Chambéry

Once upon a time, historic Chambéry was the most important city around. The **Château des Ducs de Savoie** (*Place du Château. Guided tours only: Jul–Aug Mon–Fri 10.30am, 2.30pm, 3.30pm & 4.30pm; May–Jun & Sept 2.30pm. Admission charge*), renovated after fires in the 18th century, stands as a reminder of the several centuries (13th to 16th) that Chambéry spent as capital of Savoie. Next door, the early 15th-century Sainte-Chapelle has been beautifully preserved. The castle is now administrative base for the *département*

Savoie

of Savoie, and Chambéry lacks the visitor appeal exuded by many Alpine towns. That said, this is still a convenient place to stay, due to an enviable location and useful city amenities. Lyon, Grenoble and Annecy are all fairly close, as are many high mountain resorts.

In the more immediate vicinity, pristine Alpine countryside beckons in all directions. Chambéry is an urban island in a sea of protected areas: to the south is the northern edge of the Parc Naturel Régional de Chartreuse, while to the northeast is the Parc Naturel Régional du Massif des Bauges (*see*

SAVOYARD COSTUMES

Although independent Savoie was united by some cultural traditions, each valley and village found ways to express its own unique identity. Women's costumes were an important aspect of this expression. Many of the outfits involved layering brightly coloured, elaborately designed fabric accessories, such as wide decorated belts and patterned shawls, over dark dresses. Headdresses were also popular and included white lace caps and braided velvet headbands. Jewellery was worn for weddings and celebrations. The most iconic pieces were necklaces with a heart and a cross on the same chain. Traditional Savoyard costumes are showcased at folk festivals across the region.

The remote countryside near Valloire, seen from the Col du Galibier

The beautiful countryside in northern Savoie

opposite). The proximity of the Bourget and Aiguebelette lakes makes watersports day trips feasible. Chambéry's **Maison des Parcs et de la Montagne** (*256 rue de la République. Tel: (04) 79 60 04 46. www.maisondes parcsetdelamontagne.fr. Open: Tue–Sat 10am–noon & 2–7pm*) provides information on the Vanoise, Chartreuse and Bauges parks.

Lac d'Aiguebelette

In a pretty setting just north of the Chartreuse, the Lac d'Aiguebelette is a little gem. With no motorboats allowed, it is peaceful and still, ideal for swimming, fishing and rowing. Thanks to its clean water and reed marshes,

Aiguebelette has a thriving ecosystem of fish and birds.

Parc Naturel Régional du Massif des Bauges

The Massif des Bauges is a vast patch of Alpine countryside between Chambéry, Annecy and Albertville. There are some high summits in the centre, but in general the landscape is made up of lower hills, cliffs, plateaux and valleys. The park protects a diverse wildlife, including chamois and moufflons. In the east of the massif, Mont Revard offers a spectacular panorama over the Lac du Bourget, plus a view of Mont Blanc in the other direction.

Drive: Col de l'Iseran and Col du Mont Cenis

This route, traversing two high mountain passes, is only possible between early summer and autumn as there is too much snow at other times (part of the road actually doubles up as a ski piste!). It passes through the peripheral zone of the Parc National de la Vanoise and the spectacular landscapes alter wildly with the changes in altitude.

Allow two hours for the drive, plus short stops at each point, or the best part of a day to include lingering at the viewpoints and walking along trails.

Start at Val d'Isère.

1 Val d'Isère

If you are not staying in the village already, it is worth a wander around. The tourist office has village tour maps. For picnic supplies, try the bakery on the main street.

Summer in Val d'Isère

Take the D902 out of the village in the direction of the Col de l'Iseran.

2 Pont Saint-Charles

This little bridge across the river is a good starting point for walking trails in the area. There is a car park just before the bridge.

About 11km (7 miles) after Val d'Isère is a right turn signed 'Lac d'Ouillette', leading to a car park a few minutes' walk from the lake, which is also accessible via Val's Solaise chairlift.

3 Lac de l'Ouillette

This pretty mountain lake is a popular fishing spot.

Returning to the main road, continue for less than 1km (½ mile) and look out for a small wooden hut and car park on the right. The viewing tables are across the road, a short walk uphill.

4 Tables d'orientation géologiques

Information points do not get much more beautiful than these works of art painted on marble. The circular and semicircular 'geological orientation tables' depict and label the peaks you see all around.

The road continues to climb for another few kilometres.

5 Col de l'Iseran

This is the highest road in Europe (2,764m/9,070ft) and the meeting point of the upper Tarentaise and Maurienne valleys. The scenery at the top is stark and dramatic, almost lunar in appearance.

14km (8½ miles) from the Col de l'Iseran you will reach the village of Bonneval-sur-Arc. There is a car park just off the main road where you will need to leave the car, as the village is pedestrianised.

6 Bonneval-sur-Arc

The cobblestone village of Bonneval makes an endearing introduction to the Haute-Maurienne and is a good place to stop for lunch if you haven't brought a picnic.

Continue to the village of Lanslevillard, take a left on to the D115 and then another left on to the D1006, both signed to the Col du Mont Cenis. The road winds uphill through pine forest; less than 10km (6 miles) to the Col.

7 Col du Mont Cenis

At 2,083m (6,834ft), the views from this pass are superb.

Continue on the road for about another 1.5km (just under 1 mile) to reach the lake.

8 Lac du Mont Cenis

This reservoir lake has a beautiful setting. Alpine flowers flourish in Le Jardin Alpin du Mont Cenis, a small park on the side of the lake (*Free admission*).

Continuing on the D1006 would soon take you across the border into Italy. To get back to Val d'Isère it is necessary to retrace the route as there is no short, circular option.

Drive: Col de l'Iseran and Col du Mont Cenis

The House of Savoie

A remote but strategically important mountain realm, an ambitious dynasty and almost a thousand years of feuds, invasions and alliances... the historical tale of Savoie has a fascinating and convoluted plot. Part of France only for the past 150 years, the region's unique cultural development was shaped by its long history as an independent state. In the early 11th century, the House of Savoie was founded by Humbert I. Initially a modest state, Savoie expanded stealthily through the generations thanks to some strategic royal marriages. About 400 years on from its humble beginnings, Savoie became a duchy when Amadeus VIII was made a duke by the Holy Roman Emperor in 1416 and absorbed Piedmont, in present-day Italy, into its realm. So began the era of the Dukes of Savoie, who employed complex feudal tactics and struck political bargains over the following centuries to hold on to or regain control of the land in the face of invasions by their powerful neighbours. In the mid-16th century, Duke Emmanuel-Philibert recovered Savoie from the French, who had occupied it, by temporarily teaming up with the Netherlands and

Spain and helping stir up a European storm to distract France. He then moved the Savoyard capital from Chambéry to Turin. Despite further occupations by France, the House of Savoie grew steadily stronger, to the point of invading the southern Alps in the late 17th century. This event precipitated Vauban's building of famous fortresses throughout the region, including the Vieille Ville of Briançon. In 1713, Victor-Amadeus II got to add a new title to the family collection when he was made king of Sicily by the Treaty of Utrecht, and quickly swapped Sicily for Sardinia. Savoie remained part of the Kingdom of Sardinia until 1860, apart from an interlude of post-Revolution French occupation between 1792 and 1815. King Victor-Emmanuel II of Sardinia, the last Duke of Savoie, gave up his ancestral lands in a political move: he needed French assistance to defeat the Austrians, who were occupying part of Italy, and France wanted Savoie in return.

The ultimate decision on unification with France was handed to the Savoyard people in the referendum of April 1860. While the dukes had been feuding with everyone in sight, losing, regaining and expanding their lands in the process, the ordinary people of Savoie led a largely simple, rural lifestyle. Due to the harsh winters, many young Savoyard men had been forced to emigrate to France to work at manual jobs, so they had witnessed the wealth of their neighbour. The Catholic Church was a strong presence in Savoie, but the Piedmont government was trying to instigate anticlerical policies, which set the clergy firmly in favour of France. Under these influences and with a communal sense of having been marginalised by their leadership, the people almost universally decided that France was the more attractive option. Savoie and Piedmont, although sharing much cultural and linguistic overlap, were now separated. Less than a year later, Victor-Emmanuel II (aided all the way by the ambitious Piedmont governor, Camillo di Cavour) saw his bargain pay off when he was made king of the sparkling new Kingdom of Italy. The ancestral House of Savoie continued in its promoted role as the Italian monarchy until the abdication of Umberto II in 1946 finally ended the thousand-year-old dynasty.

The Château de Ripaille where Amadeus VIII used to reside

Haute-Savoie

In a land of contrasts, Haute-Savoie stands head and shoulders above the rest. This is the site of Alpine giant Mont Blanc, provider of extreme sports and extreme views. At the other end of the spectrum are the mountain-fringed lakes of Geneva (Lac Léman) and Annecy, where the scenery is also distinctive but more serene. Mountain resorts, meandering valleys, traditional villages and hilltop castles all add to the region's diverse appeal.

Haute-Savoie is the northern part of the old Savoyard realm and elements of the region's heritage survive in the architecture and culture here as in neighbouring Savoie. Popular and historic Annecy makes a lovely introduction to the area and an idyllic destination for lakeside wanderings and watersports. Lac Léman is equally suited to tranquil summer strolling and cruising.

Visitors looking for higher-adrenalin activities will want to head up to the heights. The biggest (in both senses) attraction is Mont Blanc, coupled with the famous town of Chamonix, which provides a winter and summer base for exploring the mountain. A holiday destination since the 19th century, Chamonix secured a place in sporting history by hosting the first winter Olympics in 1924.

Throughout the region there are various other locations in which to indulge in both winter and summer activities, from several smaller resorts in the shadow of Mont Blanc to the vast Portes du Soleil area, which, centred on the town of Morzine, is made up of a network of ski pistes in winter, transformed into hiking and mountain-bike trails for the summer season.

MASSIF DU MONT BLANC

The tallest mountain in the European Union forms part of a magnificent glacial wall of sky-scraping peaks along the French–Italian border. These mountains represent Alpine scenery at its most awe-inspiring. Although much of the high ground is inaccessible except to experienced mountaineers, round trips by cable car make it possible for everyone to enjoy breathtaking summit views.

Chamonix

There are many sides to Chamonix, a town which has been in the limelight for a long time thanks to its position at the foot of Mont Blanc. Part serious

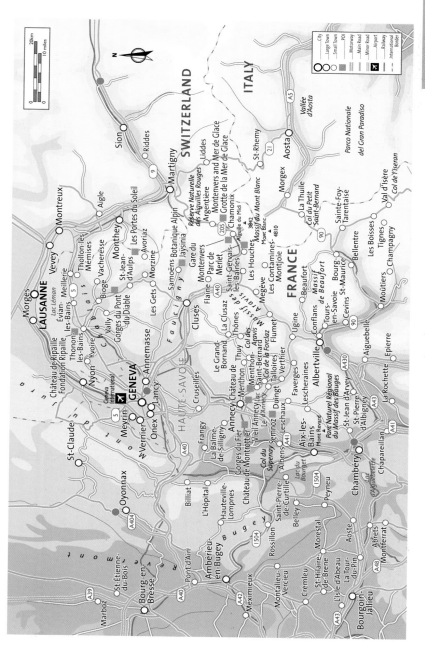

mountaineering centre, part lively tourist resort and part historical Alpine town, Chamonix has a unique charisma. It can seem overcrowded at times, but all the international visitors and residents contribute to the cosmopolitan atmosphere and happening nightlife. This is one of the few mountain destinations that welcomes visitors year-round. The town is arranged around the river Arve at the heart of the Vallée de Chamonix, which divides the Mont Blanc and Aiguilles Rouges massifs. Place Balmat and the pedestrian streets branching off it are at the centre of the action, with plentiful restaurants, bars and shops. An array of sporting and cultural events plus festivals in summer and winter add to the town's party reputation.

As a winter sports destination, Chamonix is best suited to the more expert end of the spectrum. Local guides are on hand to introduce competent adrenalin-seekers to some fantastic off-piste terrain. There are more mainstream pistes too, but they are scattered around, and getting from one sector to another takes time. In summer, Chamonix has more of an all-round appeal, with an exhaustive list of activities and attractions to enjoy. Anyone planning to visit two or more of the key sites should consider purchasing a Mont Blanc MultiPass, which covers the Aiguille du Midi, Mont Blanc Tramway, Montenvers-Mer de Glace and other cable cars. Adult MultiPasses cost €49.50 for one day and significantly decreasing amounts

Aiguille de Rochefort and Les Grandes Jorasses in the Massif du Mont Blanc

THE COMPAGNIE DES GUIDES

Following the first successful ascent of Mont Blanc in 1786, more and more explorers were drawn to the legendary mountain, formerly considered haunted and inaccessible. After one particularly disastrous expedition by a scientist who failed to heed avalanche warnings, a group of local guides teamed up to improve mountain safety. The result was the Compagnie des Guides, founded in 1821 to train and protect the rights of professional guides. Today, having paved the way for other guide organisations across the Alps, the original company is still going strong, with some 200 guides based at its Chamonix office. Visitors looking for guided tours of the mountain are in good hands.

for subsequent days (for example, €55 for two). They are available from local **ticket offices** (*Tel: (04) 50 53 22 75. www.compagniedumontblanc.fr*). As well as information, Chamonix's **Office de Tourisme** also has Wi-Fi for laptop-users (*Place du Triangle de l'Amitié. Tel: (04) 50 53 00 24. www.chamonix.com*).

Aiguille du Midi

The lofty granite needle of the Aiguille du Midi (3,842m/12,604ft) rises spectacularly above Chamonix and is linked to the town by the most famous cable car in the Alps. Divided into two sections, the route has a halfway stop at the Plan de l'Aiguille (2,317m/7,601ft). From here, the Grand Balcon Nord (Great North Balcony) walking trail traverses the mountains to Montenvers (a two- or three-hour trip). There are also a couple of downhill walking trails

leading back to Chamonix. A second cable car continues up to the summit of the Aiguille du Midi, where there is a series of panoramic platforms with outstanding views. Climb the steps between the platforms slowly in case you feel altitude effects. Warm clothes are important at all times, as even in the height of summer the temperature is generally below or only narrowly above freezing. At peak times, especially July and August, the Aiguille du Midi attracts very long queues. Getting there early in the morning is a way to beat most of the crowds.
Tel: (04) 50 53 30 80/(04) 50 53 22 75. Open: Apr–Jun & early Sept 7 or 8am–5.30pm; Jul–Aug 6.30am–6pm; late Sept–Oct & late Dec–Mar 8.30am–4.30pm. Admission charge.

An aerial view of Chamonix from the Aiguille du Midi

Chamonix town centre

Montenvers and Mer de Glace

Pioneering tourist William Windham described the Montenvers glacier in 1741 as 'a sort of agitated sea that seemed suddenly to have become frozen', inspiring its name: 'Mer de Glace' means 'Sea of Ice'. Since 1908, a steep mountain railway has connected Montenvers to Chamonix, making the Mer de Glace easily accessible. The route's old-fashioned red train is an attraction in itself, but the main points of interest are at the top of the line. From the Montenvers station (1,913m/6,276ft), access to the glacier is via a short cable-car ride and a staircase. At the bottom of the steps is the ephemeral **Grotte de la Mer de Glace** (*Open: mid-Dec–Apr & Jun–Sept*), an ice cave carved into the glacier. Inside, light displays illuminate the ice, and posters recount the glacier's story. As the glacier is moving incredibly quickly, a new ice cave is created every year – the old entrances are visible from the steps. Signs on the way down to the cave also track the glacier's currently retreating path. There is a small exhibit of crystals by the top railway station. In Chamonix, the **Gare du Montenvers** (*Tel: (04) 50 53 12 54. www.compagniedu montblanc.com. Open: Jul–Aug 8am–6.30pm; mid-Dec–Apr 9am–4.30pm; rest of the year variable. Train fare includes entrance to ice cave*) is located behind the main train station.

Argentière and Aiguilles Rouges

The resort of Argentière, located 9km (5½ miles) up the valley from Chamonix on the slopes of the Massif des Aiguilles Rouges, is a base for the ski area of Les Grands Montets and also for summer excursions. Above

Argentière, the Réserve Naturelle des Aiguilles Rouges (Aiguilles Rouges Nature Reserve) extends to 2,995m (9,826ft) and protects mountain animals and varied Alpine plants. There is a **Chalet d'Accueil information centre** (*Tel: (04) 50 54 08 06*) on the Col des Montets and a nature trail.

Les Houches

Six kilometres (3¾ miles) south of Chamonix is the village of Les Houches, which provides a more restful family-friendly alternative. It has a ski area, good facilities and wonderful views of the Mont Blanc massif. The village's **Parc de Merlet** enables visitors to see Alpine animals in an attractive woodland setting (*Tel: (04) 50 53 47 89. www.parcdemerlet.com. Open: Jul–Aug 9.30am–7.30pm; May–Jun & Sept 10am–6pm. Admission charge*).

Megève

Sophisticated Megève has been an ultra-fashionable place to ski since the 1920s. The oldest sections of the village are medieval and the whole centre is pretty as a picture thanks to its cobbled pedestrianised streets, horse-drawn sledges, elegant church and boutique shops. Megève's ski area is linked to that of nearby Saint-Gervais-les-Bains and a few mini-stations to form the Évasion-Mont Blanc area (adult pass €36.50 one-day, €176 six-day), which has 445km (275 miles) of pistes. The slopes above Megève are scenic and leisurely, but the resort caters largely to a smart, moneyed crowd and lacks widespread winter appeal. Summer is a different story, with a more all-inclusive atmosphere and good mountain activities.

Saint-Gervais-les-Bains

Saint-Gervais is a well-connected town, with a cable-car link to the ski area of Évasion-Mont Blanc and a mountain railway (*see p94*) providing access to an incredible glacial landscape. Saint-Gervais is also the main spa town of the Mont Blanc massif and a welcoming and convenient place to stay.

The illuminated ice cave inside the Mer de Glace

Walk: Grand Balcon Sud (Great Southern Balcony)

This is a route for a clear day, as it is all about the views of peaks and glaciers. It includes a long section of the Grand Balcon Sud, one of the classic hiking routes in the vicinity of Mont Blanc.

The main hike covers a distance of about 6km (3¾ miles), takes about two hours and requires a moderate level of fitness. Although the altitude is virtually constant, there is some meandering up and down hill. Allow half a day to include round trips on the extra chairlift and cable car.

Start at the bottom of the Flégère chairlift in the Les Praz area. Les Praz can be reached by bus or train from Chamonix.

1 La Flégère
As the cable car climbs, there is a superb view of the Mer de Glace and Montenvers opposite. From the top, you can see the distinctive outline of the Mont Blanc range with its *aiguilles*

The famous cable car

(needles), *pointes* (points) and *dents* (teeth).
At the cable-car station (1,894m/ 6,214ft), transfer to the Index chairlift to go up to the summit.

2 L'Index
From up here at 2,396m (7,861ft), the views are even better. There are two walking trails from the summit, but both are long routes. The Lacs Noirs walk is a higher-altitude alternative to the route to Planpraz described below. The Lac Blanc trail is a walk to a glacial lake that takes about two and a half hours as a return trip.
Go back down in the chairlift to La Flégère and follow signs to Planpraz.

3 Grand Balcon Sud
Much of the walk is along a narrow path lined by Alpine plants. Some short sections are through pine forest, but most of the track is at the top of the treeline. About 15 minutes into the walk there is a short but steep staircase.

In between the wooded path there are several rockier sections, where the route crosses dry scree slopes. There is no difficulty walking across, but care should be taken.

At the couple of junctions with other paths, follow signs to Planpraz.

4 Planpraz

As you approach Planpraz (2,000m/ 6,560ft) there is a spectacular vista of the Aiguille du Midi, Mont Blanc and the other eternally snow-capped domes at the edge of the massif. The river of ice stretching down towards the valley below Mont Blanc is the Glacier des Bossons. There is also a clear view over Chamonix and the valley from this point.

Next to the upper station of the Planpraz cable car is the lower station of the Brévent cable car, which climbs about

another 500m (1,640ft). From the top cable-car station, there is a short uphill path to the summit (2,525m/8,284ft).

5 Le Brévent

A highly rewarding 360-degree panorama awaits you at the summit, with a viewing table naming the visible mountains. There is also a small mountain hut, the **Chalet d'Accueil du Brévent** (*Open: May–Sept & autumn weekends 9.30am–6pm. Free admission*), which contains large wall maps. There are other marked walking routes from here if you feel like coming back for more, and it is also possible, although lengthy, to return to Chamonix on foot. *Return to Chamonix via the Brévent and Planpraz cable cars. The town centre is about a ten-minute walk downhill from the lower Planpraz station.*

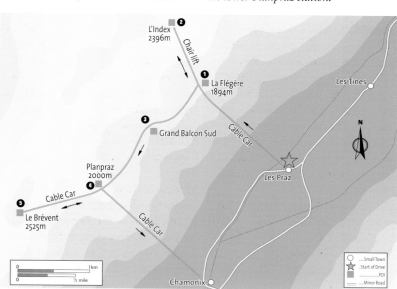

The Grand Balcon Sud on the Aiguilles Rouges side of the valley

Tramway du Mont Blanc

France's highest rack railway ascends over 1,500m (4,920ft) from Saint-Gervais and nearby Le-Fayet through layers of changing Alpine scenery to the Nid d'Aigle (Eagle's Nest) at 2,380m (7,808ft). From the top, there is a spectacular view of the Bionassay glacier. Mountaineers climbing Mont Blanc often start here. In winter, the route is shortened and only goes as far as Bellevue (1,800m/ 5,905ft).

80 avenue de la Gare, Le Fayet/571 rue du Mont-Lachat, Saint-Gervais.
Tel: (04) 50 47 51 83.
www.compagniedumontblanc.com.
Open: mid-Dec–Apr & mid-Jun–Sept.
Admission charge.

Les Contamines-Montjoie

Part of the Évasion ski area, Les Contamines is a smaller, less showy and less pricey alternative to nearby Megève. It has an authentic village square, a reasonably varied collection of ski pistes and plenty of summer hiking trails.

ANNECY AND LAC D'ANNECY

Known as the Venice of the Alps, regional capital Annecy has a distinct magnetism concentrated in the centuries-old district at the town's heart, a jumble of canals, cobblestone streets and graceful old buildings in a mixture of styles from medieval to 17th century. With all this in an exquisite lakeside mountain setting, it is little wonder that Annecy draws hordes of visitors, but even in August the town feels more animatedly than unpleasantly crowded. Around the shores of the lake several smaller towns offer quieter holiday bases. The whole area is steeped in history, visible in the clutch of Savoyard castles perched around the lake. Information and maps are available at Annecy's **Office de Tourisme** (*1 rue Jean Jaurès. Tel: (04) 50 45 00 33. www.lac-annecy.com*).

Vieil Annecy

Vieil Annecy (not the same place as Annecy-le-Vieux, a nearby lakeside community) is the compact Old Town that deservedly attracts all the attention. Its extraordinary geography is based upon two narrow canals, branches of the river Thiou that runs through the town. Each of the canals is crossed by a series of little bridges leading into labyrinthine streets between and around the waterways. In the south of the Old Town, the streets become steep and lead uphill to the château.

Musée-Château (Castle Museum)

In addition to showcasing the 12th–16th-century castle, the museum has collections of Savoyard art and craft items and an exhibition dedicated to Alpine lakes.
Tel: (04) 50 33 87 30. Open: Jun–Sept 10.30am–6pm; Oct–May Wed–Mon 10am–noon & 2–5pm. Admission charge (free first Sun of month Oct–May).

Lac d'Annecy is an idyllic place to relax on a sunny day

Competing at altitude

Although the majority of visitors to the Alps take part in sports for fun, there is a competitive slant to the slopes as well. The earliest ski competitions were staged by Alpine military troops at the start of the 20th century, but it was the first ever Winter Olympic Games, held in Chamonix in 1924, that really kick-started the trend of winter sports spectacles. Two subsequent Winter Olympics have been hosted by the French Alps: the 10th in Grenoble in 1968 and the 16th in Albertville in 1992. All three Olympics had a significant and lasting influence on the venues and the region as a whole. Chamrousse, the closest ski resort to Grenoble, was developed for the 1968 Games. Olympic buildings in Grenoble itself include the Palais des Sports, a large ice-hockey arena which has since been used for several other international competitions. Leaving their mark in a different way, the 1968 Olympics also led to the naming of the Espace Killy ski area, after triple-gold medallist Jean-Claude Killy, who grew up in Val d'Isère. The 1992 Albertville Olympics saw the whole of Savoie get involved, with events held in Les Arcs, La Plagne, Courchevel, Méribel, Les Menuires, Pralognan-la-Vanoise,

Tignes, Val d'Isère and Les Saisies, boosting facilities across the *département*. Tignes and Albertville also hosted the fifth Winter Paralympics, making history as it was the first time the Winter Olympics and Paralympics had been held at the same site.

More recently, Val d'Isère, which annually hosts the first international downhill skiing competition of the season, the Critérium de la Première Neige, also scooped the 2009 FIS (International Ski Federation) Alpine World Ski Championships. Meanwhile, at Val Thorens, freestyle snowboarders and skiers compete at the annual Boarderweek festival. More unusual winter events include an annual ice sculpture competition in Valloire (*www.valloire.net*), snow polo in Megève (*www.megeve.com*) and a dog-sleigh race across Savoie and Haute-Savoie (La Grande Odyssée Savoie Mont Blanc, *www.grandeodyssee.com*).

In summer, the emphasis switches from racing down snowy slopes to racing up or down green and rocky ones. The most famous professional cycling event in the world, the Tour de France, has been passing through the Alps for around a hundred years. Although the route of the race changes every year, it typically includes arduous stages up winding mountain roads. Some of the toughest climbs used are the road up to L'Alpe d'Huez, the Col du Galibier and the Col de la Bonette. The best climber of the race wins the title King of the Mountains and gets to wear an identifying white jersey with red polka dots.

Other summer sporting events include an international climbing festival in Chamonix each July, which is part of the climbing world cup. This competition is staged on an outdoor artificial rock wall in front of a large audience, creating a festival atmosphere. Mountain-biking events take place in several resorts. The best known is the annual Mega Avalanche downhill cycling race, which descends 2,600m (8,530ft) in 33km (20 miles) from the glacial Pic Blanc (3,320m/ 10,890ft) above L'Alpe d'Huez to the little village of Allemont (720m/2,360ft).

A downhill skier competes in the slalom race in Val d'Isère

The Pont des Amours, Annecy

Palais de l'Île (sometimes also spelt Palais de l'Îsle)

This curious building marooned in the Canal du Thiou at the heart of the Old Town is Annecy's most iconic attraction. Originally a 12th-century fort, the Palais de l'Île did stints as a prison, a palace and a court before assuming its present function as a museum. Combined tickets for the palace museum and the Musée-Château d'Annecy are available.

Tel: (04) 50 33 87 30. Open: Jun–Sept 10.30am–6pm; Oct–May Wed–Mon 10am–noon & 2–5pm. Admission charge.

Annecy lakefront

Central Annecy includes two lakeside parks divided by the Canal du Vassé but linked by the romantic Pont des Amours (Lovers' Bridge). The Jardins de l'Europe are pretty landscaped gardens, while the Champ de Mars is an open green field. Several public beaches (*open Jul–Aug*) are located near the town. Just south of the Jardins de l'Europe is the Piscine des Marquisats, a swimming centre with three outdoor pools.

Talloires and Duingt

Lac d'Annecy is at its narrowest between the villages of Talloires, on the eastern shore, and Duingt, on the western shore. At Duingt, a little peninsula juts out on to the lake, crowned by the striking Château de Ruphy, or Châteauvieux (not open to the public). Scenically placed Talloires boasts a great view across to the castle, as well as a harbour, beach and watersports centre.

Le Semnoz

Starting just outside Annecy and rising above the western coast of the lake, the Semnoz is a mountainous ridge that is easily accessible from town. The summit (1,699m/5,574ft) is 18km (11 miles) south of Annecy, but there are forested walking trails much closer with lookout points over the lake.

Col de la Forclaz

An incredible vista over Lac d'Annecy makes this 1,157m (3,795ft) peak a paragliders' paradise. In high summer, flocks of brightly coloured parachutes circling above the lake are a standard feature. Other activities based up here include pony rides for children and microlight flights.

Menthon-Saint-Bernard

This likeable lakeside resort is crowned by one of the most eye-catching castles in the area. Inhabited by descendants of the same family throughout its thousand-year history, the **Château de Menthon** developed gradually from a medieval fortress into a fairy tale castle.

Château de Menthon. Tel: (04) 50 60 12 05. www.chateau-de-menthon.com. Open: Jul–Aug noon–6pm; May–Jun & Sept Fri–Sun 2–6pm. Admission charge.

Gorges du Fier and Château de Montrottier

These two sites are close to each other, about 20km (12½ miles) from Annecy, which makes a combined geological and architectural-heritage trip easy.

The Palais de l'Île in its glowing after-dark form

Visitors can walk deep into the remarkable Fier gorge along a balcony-like footbridge attached to the rock. The castle, originally a 13th-century fortress although much was added later, contains an eclectic collection of regional and international art and antiques.

Gorges du Fier. Tel: (04) 50 46 23 07. www.gorgesdufier.com. Open: mid-Mar–mid-Oct 9.30am–6.15pm (to 7.15pm mid-Jun–mid-Sept). Admission charge.

Château de Montrottier. Tel: (04) 50 46 23 02. www.chateaudemontrottier.com. Open: Jun–Aug 2–6 or 7pm; mid-Mar–May & Sept–mid-Oct Wed–Mon 2–6pm. Admission charge.

LAC LÉMAN (LAKE GENEVA)

Lac Léman forms a natural border between France and Switzerland and between the Alps and the Jura. Rolling hills at the edge of both mountain ranges extend almost to Léman's shores, affording beautiful vantage points over the vast, crescent-shaped lake.

Évian-les-Bains

Between the huge lake on the doorstep and the mountain springs in the back garden, water is a star attraction in these parts. Besides supplying the famous spring-water company, Évian is also a hydrotherapy centre and a port for ferry excursions around the lake. Lac Léman's history is explored in short excursions aboard *La Savoie*, a faithful replica of an 1896 sailboat and essentially a floating museum (*sailings Jun–mid-Sept, enquire at the tourist office for times and tickets*). Évian is a summer resort and the town practically shuts down in the winter. As well as sailing, swimming and sporting on the lake, golf and tennis are very popular.

Behind the lakefront promenade, ornate public buildings from the town's 19th-century spa heyday project sophistication. The Villa Lumière, once a holiday home of the famous cinematic family, is now the town hall, and the Palais Lumière, a former spa, is now a conference centre. Both have grand foyers open to the public and host art exhibitions. Uphill on lively Rue Nationale, the palatial Buvette de la Source Cachat, an impressive Art Nouveau building, is home to Évian water headquarters. A free funicular

railway departing from behind the Palais Lumière connects the town centre with the hills. Évian's **Office de Tourisme** is located near the waterfront (*Place d'Allinges. Tel: (04) 50 75 04 26. www.ville-evian.fr*).

Thonon-les-Bains

One of the main towns on the lake shore, Thonon has a lively atmosphere reminiscent of the seaside, boasting a large marina and a promenade lined with cafés and restaurants – unsurprisingly specialising in fish dishes. A funicular railway (€1 for a single) climbs from the marina to the town centre, where there is an attractive cluster of pedestrian streets. Opposite the lakefront funicular station is a useful tourist information kiosk.

Château de Ripaille

This impressive castle, which was built, extended and renovated in stages throughout Savoie's history, is one of the most complete in the region. The vineyards surrounding the castle are part of a thoroughly modern estate, the **Fondation Ripaille** (*Tel: (04) 50 26 64 44. www.ripaille.fr*), which produces wine, runs guided castle tours (*Feb–Nov daily, times vary*) and sponsors ecological research.

Yvoire

The amazingly well-preserved medieval centre of Yvoire has earned accolades as one of the prettiest villages in France. Cars must be left outside the arched

La Savoie, an old-style tall-ship sailing boat on Lac Léman

The grand waterfront buildings of Évian-les-Bains

entrances and the narrow cobblestone streets explored on foot. Yvoire's shoreline position, accessible along the coast road or by boat, makes it very popular with summer day-trippers. Many of the lovely stone buildings in the streets above the port now house restaurants and artisan shops.

CHABLAIS

The Chablais is the most northerly massif in the Alps, extending from the low hills by Lac Léman to the higher mountains of the Portes du Soleil area.

Les Portes du Soleil

The Haut-Chablais (Upper Chablais) is the site of the romantically named Portes du Soleil ('Gates of the Sun'), which extends across the border into Switzerland. A vast 650km (404-mile)

network of pistes connecting eight French resorts with four Swiss ones makes this the largest linked ski area in the world – as well as one of the most famous European mountain-biking destinations. Of the main French resorts, Avoriaz is on the central Portes du Soleil circuit, while Morzine and Les Gets are connected to it by lifts and roads and also have their own separate slopes. Adult lift passes for the whole area cost €40 for one day (€205 for six), but cheaper options are available for just the local resorts. In summer, the Portes du Soleil MultiPass costs just €6 a day and includes pedestrian lift access plus entrance to swimming pools, tennis courts and some other facilities. Adult mountain-bike lift passes, with the same added extras, are €20.50 (one-day) and €82 (six-day).

Walk: Annecy

This walking tour takes in the highlights of Annecy lakefront and the Old Town. The walk is about 2.5km (1½ miles) long and takes about an hour and a half at strolling pace, although with longer stops the route could easily fill half a day.

Start at the tourist office. Cross the road in front of the tourist office and walk along Promenade Jacquet, between the Champ de Mars and the canal.

1 Canal du Vassé

This short, scenic stretch of canal leading up to the Pont des Amours is lined with flower boxes and small wooden boats bobbing gently on the water.
Continue to the bridge and walk across.

2 Pont des Amours

One of Annecy's signature sights, the 'Lovers' Bridge' is lovely from all angles. The views from the bridge are of the charming canal in one direction and the lake framed by mountains in the other.
Turn left at the end of the bridge and follow the lakeside path round the park.

3 Les Jardins de l'Europe

The landscaped park is a lush oasis of greenery and bright flower arrangements. Factor in the stunning backdrop of the lake and mountains and you have an idyllic picnic spot.
Cross the main road on to Quai de Vicenza, by the Saint-François church, and turn left on to Pont Perrière for the best Palais de l'Île viewpoint.

4 Palais de l'Île

This eye-catching medieval building is also impossible to miss. Its compact size, quirky triangular shape, pointed roof and turrets make it highly photogenic.
Turn right at the end of the bridge on to Quai des Vieilles Prisons, walk along next to the Palais, turn left, then cross Place des Efléchères and walk up the Rampe du Château to Place du Château. The walk up to the castle is steep, but it can be left out of the route by taking Rue de l'Île and Rue Sainte-Claire straight to the Rue de la République.

5 Musée-Château

An arched tunnel from Place du Château leads into a spacious courtyard. The castle's drawn-out patchwork development accounts for the differing styles lining the courtyard, from the chunky 12th-century tower on the right of the entrance to the white 16th-century building on the left.
There are several routes back downhill. The Chemin des Remparts from opposite

the museum is quite direct. Turn right on Rue Sainte-Claire and then left on to Rue de la République.

6 Rue de la République

This road bridges both of Annecy's canals and is therefore a good vantage point for admiring the flower-bedecked quays and bridges.

After crossing the second canal, turn right on Quai Madame de Warens, cross back over the canal at the next bridge and turn left on to Quai Cathédrale.

7 Cathédrale Saint-Pierre and Église Notre-Dame-de-Liesse

The Quai Cathédrale and the canal lie between two of Annecy's four old churches: Notre-Dame-de-Liesse to the

north and Saint-Pierre to the south. The high concentration of churches is a distinctive aspect of the Old Town. Église Saint-Maurice and Église Saint-François, both opposite the Jardins de l'Europe, are the other two.

Turn right at the end of the quay on to Rue Filaterie.

8 Rue Filaterie

This is an interesting shopping street, characteristic of old Annecy. The shops include a vibrant florist and a couple of gourmet food outlets selling local specialities.

Turn left at Rue Grenette and immediately right on to Passage de l'Île and you will be back at the Palais de l'Île.

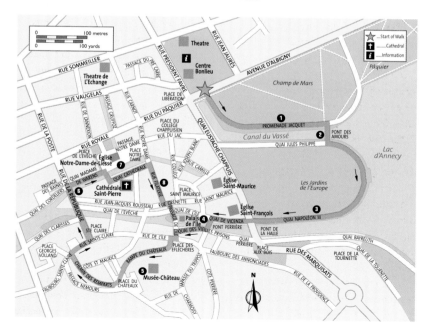

Avoriaz

Avoriaz is a purpose-built ski resort with a high originality quotient. It is car-free in winter, so horse-drawn sleighs provide an enchanting alternative. Small luggage sledges are also available for hire. Also distinctive is the cliff-top ledge setting, which inspired the quirky architecture. Although high-rise apartment blocks are typical of 1960s ski resorts, in Avoriaz they were uniquely designed using wood cladding to mimic the rocky backdrop. With a resort height of 1,800m (5,905ft), the local slopes typically get plenty of snow and there are runs to suit all abilities. Avoriaz is not as attractive as Morzine in summer, however there are good sports facilities, including a stunningly situated golf course and faux-beach volleyball. The Mosettes chairlift enables pedestrians and cyclists to ascend to 2,200m

HYDROTHERAPY

'Taking the waters' has ebbed and flowed in popularity over almost 2,000 years. It started with the Romans, who discovered the potential of mountain springs at Aix-les-Bains and Digne-les-Bains, among other places. The Dukes of Savoie later frequented the baths of the Lac Léman area. Nineteenth-century spa fashion ushered in a new golden age for Aix and Évian-les-Bains in particular. Today, the spas of the many 'Les Bains' towns of the French Alps play a major role in the leisure and wellness industries. Besides the pleasure of taking a soak, hydrotherapy has known medicinal properties and is used to treat ailments including digestive problems, rheumatism and respiratory conditions.

(7,220ft). There is an **Office de Tourisme** on Place Centrale (*Tel: (04) 50 74 02 11. www.avoriaz.com*).

Les Gets

Les Gets shares an area of ski slopes and mountain-bike trails with Morzine,

Medieval houses adorned with flowers line the streets of Yvoire

The distinctive architecture of Avoriaz

but the character of this village is very different to its higher-profile neighbours. Many of the activities in the resort are designed for families and young children, such as visits to farms, a chocolate workshop and nature trails. Details are available at the **Office de Tourisme** (*Place de la Mairie. Tel: (04) 50 75 80 80. www.lesgets.com*).

Morzine

As the main town of the Haut-Chablais, Morzine has a life and a character away from the ski slopes. It is busiest in winter, with a dynamic après-ski scene, but summers are spirited as well and there is just about no Alpine activity that cannot be experienced here. Morzine is particularly popular with mountain bikers because of its fantastic network of trails and bike parks. The trails vary greatly in length and difficulty and include challenging downhill runs, gentle circuits and a long-distance tour of the whole Portes du Soleil. Walkers also have many trails to explore, leading from the town and from the tops of the cable cars. Caution should be exercised on narrow paths shared by walkers and cyclists. From the top of the Super-Morzine chairlift, there is a magnificent panorama above the treeline. Other highlights include several lakes and waterfalls. In winter, the local ski slopes are picturesque and mainly of moderate steepness, although there are some more challenging pistes.

Most of the in-town sports facilities are located along the river, while shops and restaurants are concentrated in the lively area around the Place de l'Office du Tourisme. Besides advising on the usual sports and services, the **Office de Tourisme** (*Tel: (04) 50 74 72 72. www.morzine.com*) has information on more unusual cultural activities, including tours of the Old Town, cheese-making demonstrations at the Fruitière de Morzine and visits to a local slate workshop. Morzine is not a compact town, nor a flat one. Its attractive river gorge location does make walking from one side of town to another quite a trek, although there is a comprehensive bus network.

Gorges du Pont du Diable

Between Thonon-les-Bains and Morzine, the 'Devil's Bridge' gorges are a dazzling work of nature. The gorges take their name from a large stone archway between the cliffs. Although visitors cannot walk along the actual devil's bridge, a cliff-side balcony path gives a great view.
Tel: (04) 50 72 10 39. www.lepontdu diable.com. Open: late Apr–Sept 9am–6pm. Admission charge.

Thollon-les-Mémises

Situated 13km (8 miles) uphill from Évian, the tiny ski resort of Thollon-les-Mémises perfectly overlooks Lac Léman. Walking paths lead down to the lake from the resort and around the nearby peaks from the cable car, which is open in July and August, as well as in the ski season. The Pic des Mémises, only about 70m (230ft) higher than the top cable-car station and an easy walk, has one of the best viewpoints.

MASSIF DES ARAVIS

The Aravis is a peaceful mid-sized range between the major attractions of Annecy and Mont Blanc. Limestone

LOOK OUT FOR THE DAHU!

Children growing up in the Alps and the Jura know all about the dahu (or dahut). This elusive nocturnal creature is similar to a mountain goat or deer, but it is distinguished by one crucial feature: its legs are shorter on one side than on the other. The dahu's lopsided anatomy is a brilliant adaptation to living on steep mountainsides, as long as it only ever walks in one direction. Dahu hunts were popular in the 19th century and more recently became a summer camp activity, but oddly enough nobody has ever seen one. A few guides, such as Damien Trombert in Morzine (*www.rando-morzine.com*), still help keen visitors try their luck.

mountains, flower-filled meadows, dairy pastures and classic villages combine to create beautiful landscapes. A highlight is the Col des Aravis, from where there is a stunning summer view of Mont Blanc's white dome behind all the green. Four ski resorts – La Clusaz and Le Grand-Bornand (*see below*), plus the smaller Manigod and Saint-Jean-de-Sixt – are linked by the Espace Aravis (adult six-day passes for €146–160), with 220km (137 miles) of downhill pistes and varied cross-country terrain.

La Clusaz

La Clusaz has become the main sports resort in the Aravis without losing its authentic rural charm. Chalet-style buildings, wild-flower displays and pine trees make the village pretty, while an assortment of summer and winter activities makes it lively. Find information at the **Office de Tourisme**

(*161 place de l'Église. Tel: (04) 50 32 65 00. www.laclusaz.com*).

Le Grand-Bornand

Another rustic Aravis village turned ski resort, Le Grand-Bornand is a quiet, family-oriented place. In summer, in addition to superb hiking around the massif, it features a riverside leisure area including a swimming pool, tennis and volleyball courts and crazy golf.

LE FAUCIGNY

The pleasant Faucigny region lies at the geographical heart of Haute-Savoie. It is known for a long tradition of clock-making, based in the busy town of Cluses, as well as for the historic medieval town of La Roche-sur-Foron. In winter, the resort of Flaine and traditional village Samoëns (*see below*) combine with quieter Les Carroz and Morillon to form the large ski area of Le Grand Massif (adult lift passes €40 one-day, €204 six-day).

Flaine

Purpose-built at 1,600m (5,250ft), Flaine gets dependable snow. The modern apartment blocks that make up much of the resort are a bit of an eyesore, but they do provide good-value self-catering accommodation and the resort is conveniently compact. With an impressively well-balanced web of piste colours, Flaine has widespread appeal. It actively welcomes families and provides plenty of facilities for children.

'Village in bloom' La Clusaz

Samoëns

Stonemasonry is a traditional craft of Samoëns and the village has numerous classic stone houses showcasing this heritage. There is also a wealth of gourmet Savoyard food shops clustered in the lovely village centre. The hillside **Jardin Botanique Alpin Jaÿsinia** (*Tel: (04) 50 34 49 86. Open: May–Sept 8am–noon & 1.30–7pm; Oct–Apr 8am–noon & 1.30–4.30pm. Free admission*) is set above the village. As well as an impressive assortment of Alpine plants, the botanical gardens contain some little waterfalls. Larger waterfalls are located 13km (8 miles) from Samoëns at the Cirque du Fer à Cheval ('Horseshoe Circus'), an almost circular limestone ridge awash with streaming torrents. Other feasible summer day trips include canoeing and walking in the Giffre valley.

Haute-Savoie

Mountain cheeses

At the end of a long day in the mountains walking, skiing, cycling or working up an appetite in any of the many other available ways, a hearty cheese-centred Alpine meal has what it takes to satisfy many a craving. Whether melted in a fondue, melting in a raclette or perched on a bed of crisp salad, *fromage* plays a starring role on menus throughout the region. Dairy farming is one of the oldest industries in the Alps and making inventive use of the produce is a mainstay of the culinary culture. Different types of cheese are developed across the different valleys, so most cheeses are firmly rooted in a sense of place. Many of the varieties still around today have centuries-old pedigrees and bear the prestigious *Appellation d'Origine Contrôlée* (AOC, 'label of inspected origin'). Cheeses are still produced in the traditional way at high-altitude dairies in storybook chalet buildings, as well as in *fruitières* (cheese cooperatives) in towns throughout the mountains. A number of such places open their doors to visitors to show how their cheeses are made and provide tasting sessions. Most supermarkets also have a good selection at their deli counters, although for sheer variety you can't beat a *fromagerie* (specialist cheese shop). The heritage of Alpine cheeses is celebrated and promoted throughout the region with events, guided tours and even themed walking routes. In Savoie, **l'Association des Fromages Traditionnels des Alpes Savoyardes** (*Tel: (04) 50 32 74 79. www.fromagesdesavoie.fr, in French*) has details, as do local tourist offices. A comprehensive cheese board of local favourites would include:

- Abondance – originating from the Abondance valley in the Chablais and made from the milk of Abondance cows, this solid but creamy cheese has a pedigree dating from the Middle Ages.
- Banon – a *fromage de chèvre* (goat's cheese) from the Alpes-de-Haute-Provence. It comes distinctively wrapped in chestnut leaves and has a strong taste due to a long fermentation.
- Beaufort – this richly flavoured fromage *à pâté dure* (hard cheese) is a type of Gruyère, with a mellow, fruity taste. It hails from the high Alpine heartland of the Beaufortain and Tarentaise areas.

- Bleu de Termignon – a *fromage à pâté persillée* (blue cheese) from the high mountain pastures, which is produced only by a handful of farms today.
- Chevrotin – a goat's cheese made from the milk of the mountain breed of goat.
- Comté – a hard cow's milk cheese produced in the Jura mountains, but popular in the Alps as well.
- Reblochon de Savoie – there are two types of this strong-tasting, nutty, creamy cheese: *laitier* (made in dairies) and *fermier* (made directly on farms). Both hail from the Thônes valley in the Aravis region, where the cheese has been produced since the 13th century.
- Saint-Marcellin – a traditional Dauphiné *fromage à pâté molle* (soft cheese), made nowadays from a blend of goat's and cow's milk
- Tomme de Savoie – the most famous *tomme* ('cheese' in Savoyard dialect) is a *fromage à pâté demi-dure*, or semi-hard uncooked cheese, made from cow's milk. The word 'Savoie' is printed on the edge of the rounds, making it easily identifiable.
- Vacherin Mont d'Or – a soft nutty cheese from the Jura, known as 'hot box cheese' because it is traditionally baked in foil with white wine, onions and garlic and then eaten hot out of the foil case.

Tommes de Savoie on display

Southern Alps

As the Alps reach southwards, the cultures and ecosystems of the mountains combine with those of Provençal and Mediterranean France, creating a distinctive and enthralling region. The sun usually shines on this area, showing off the snow-capped peaks, sparkling lakes and rugged natural parks to best effect. There are no large urban centres here, just compact towns and romantic perched villages.

Both less populated and less visited than more northerly parts, the southern Alps are a tempting destination for travellers looking to holiday a little further away from the beaten track. The main towns of the region are Briançon, Gap, Digne-les-Bains and Sisteron, all of which boast convenient access to the great outdoors all around.

With a large chunk of the Écrins National Park, and all of the Mercantour National Park and the Queyras Regional Park within the area, fans of Alpine wilderness will find much to enjoy. Although the internationally best-known French ski stations are concentrated further north, the Hautes-Alpes area boasts some excellent slopes, and several small resorts in Alpes-Maritimes offer opportunities to ski remarkably close to the Riviera. Summer activities are also widely available, including watersports on the large Serre-Ponçon lake and no shortage of walking trails.

Administratively there are three parts to the southern Alps: Hautes-Alpes is the link between Isère and Savoie to the north, and Alpes-de-Haute-Provence and Alpes-Maritimes are at the edge of the mountains. The Alps stop just short of the coast, leading to spectacular views over the Côte d'Azur from the most southerly parts.

HAUTES-ALPES

High mountain passes, wild protected areas and off-the-radar valleys are the signature landscapes of Hautes-Alpes. Between the remote Écrins and Queyras parks and the Italian border, the mountainous Briançonnais region contains the ski resorts of Serre-Chevalier and Montgenèvre. Further south, the main attraction is the Lac de Serre-Ponçon.

Briançon

The historic capital of the Briançonnais region was strategically founded on a rocky plateau at the junction of four

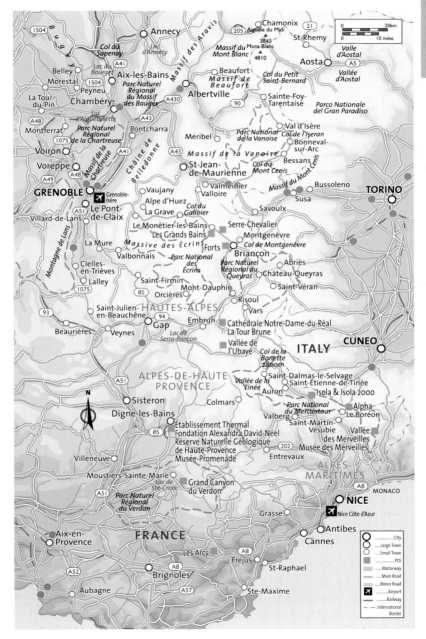

valleys, at a lofty elevation of 1,320m (4,330ft). Above the centre of modern Briançon is the town's crowning glory, the fortified Vieille Ville (Old Town), a labyrinth of sloping cobbled streets within impressive ramparts. Briançon is a place for feeling healthy and full of vitality: the air is clear, the sun shines most of the time and the steep streets provide warm-up opportunities for adventures in the nearby Serre-Chevalier valley and Écrins National Park. Fortunately, the local restaurants are on hand to deal with the big appetites worked up by the exercise. Hearty traditional specialities combined with Italian and international influences lead to some intriguing menu choices. Six restaurants across town serve *menus Vauban*, featuring 17th-century recipes in honour of the famous architect. There is little of interest in the modern town beyond the usual conveniences. Rue Centrale is the main thoroughfare.

Forts

Five forts overlook Briançon. Four of them (Fort des Salettes, Fort du Dauphin, Fort des Têtes and Fort du Randouillet) are to the east of the Old Town, separated from it by parkland and modern roads. The fifth, Fort du Château, is at the top of the Vieille Ville and there is a signed footpath up. It is quite an uphill trek, but the reward is impressive views of the jagged peaks of the Écrins Massif.

Vieille Ville

The Old Town is also called the Cité Vauban (Vauban City), in recognition

The landscape of the Hautes-Alpes has a vivid colour scheme

VAUBAN

Royally appointed military engineer Sébastien le Prestre de Vauban (1633–1707) was a man on a mission to fortify France. He served Louis XIV for 50 years, during which time he built fortresses across the country. Recognising Dauphiné's vulnerability to potential attacks from Italy and Savoie, he set out to work with the mountain terrain to select the optimal sites and devise uniquely adapted defences for each one. The pioneering fortifications he built at Briançon, Mont-Dauphin (near the town of Guillestre), Entrevaux, Colmars and Château-Queyras are standing strong to this day. Along with ten of Vauban's other works across France, Briançon and Mont-Dauphin were recently made UNESCO World Heritage Sites.

of its famous architect (*see box*). Four gates (Porte Dauphin, Porte de Pignerol, Porte d'Embrun and Porte de la Durance) give access to the walled-in section. Drawing large numbers of visitors, the Vieille Ville is usually a hive of activity, especially along the main street, Grande Rue. Watch out for the drain that runs like a stream right down the middle of this street. It is one of several mini canals, also known as *gargouilles* (gargoyles), in the area. They were built hundreds of years ago to supply water for fire fighting and are now used for watering plants.

Place d'Armes and Place du Temple are the main squares. Vibrant Place d'Armes, lined by pavement cafés, has a Provençal feel to it, despite the high altitude. Place du Temple is the location of the **Office du Tourisme** (*Tel: (04) 92 21 08 50. www.briancon.com &*

www.serre-chevalier.com), which provides information on the whole of Serre-Chevalier. Also on the square is the Collégiale Notre-Dame et Saint-Nicholas, a church designed by Vauban, which has a lovely old sundial on its southern side. Other sundials are located on the Église des Cordeliers and the Maison du Roi on Place d'Armes.

Serre-Chevalier

Serre-Chevalier is a ski area linked to Briançon via the Télécabine du Prorel (*Avenue René Froger*) and also connected to the valley villages of Le Monêtier-les-Bains, Villeneuve and Chantemerle. Part of the area's charm is that it is based on traditional villages rather than purpose-built resorts. Serre-Chevalier can accommodate all levels of ability, with 250km (155 miles)

Briançon's military connection is showcased on Place d'Armes

of pistes split between these four interlinking sectors. The resorts all have main access lifts up to over 2,000m (6,560ft) and many of the peaks are at around 2,500–2,700m (8,200–8,860ft). Winter lift passes cost €41.50 for one day, €199.50 for six. There are nursery slopes in every sector and lots of long pretty woodland runs perfect for intermediate cruising. A good range of alternative winter sports includes picturesque cross-country tracks through the valley, snowshoe circuits round the mountains and ice rinks in each of the centres. In summer, lifts run from each resort and walking trails lead back down. Tired limbs can be soothed at **Les Grands Bains**, an inexpensive hot spring centre in Le Monêtier-les-Bains (*Tel: (04) 92 40 00 00. www.lesgrandsbains.fr*).

Briançon's lively Grand Rue

HANNIBAL'S ALPINE CROSSING

The French Alps were a stage in one of the most famous journeys in antiquity: Carthaginian commander Hannibal's overland march from Iberia to Italy in 218 BC. Hannibal's epic trek across the Alps accompanied by an army of men and elephants is legendary, but nobody is sure exactly which route he took. Historians have three main contenders: the Col de Montgenèvre, the Col du Mont-Cenis or the Col du Petit Saint-Bernard. Route details aside, the journey is known to have been tortuous. Opting for the perils of the mountains was the lynchpin of Hannibal's strategic genius, giving him the advantage of surprise over the Romans.

Montgenèvre

In winter, frontier town Montgenèvre (just 2km/1¼ miles from Italy) is one of the satellite ski resorts in the sprawling Franco-Italian Voie Lactée/Via Lattea (Milky Way) network. It is possible to ski from here to Clavière in Italy, but a car is necessary to explore the other Italian resorts. Within Montgenèvre there are plenty of pistes to keep intermediate and novice skiers happy and the woodland setting is lovely. Snowfall tends to be ample and luckily clear days are typical too, showing off the resort at its glittering best. The small Old Town is welcoming and the atmosphere is cheerful. Montgenèvre's potential as a ski centre was discovered over a hundred years ago. It was here, in 1901, that French downhill skiing was essentially born. Summer sports are offered too, with a swimming pool, climbing and trails for hiking and mountain biking.

Embrun

Embrun is visited primarily as the main town around the Lac de Serre-Ponçon. However, the town long predates the creation of the lake, with a history of regional importance and influence going back to Roman times. Embrun's medieval Cathédrale Notre-Dame-du-Réal was the seat of powerful regional archbishops and a popular pilgrimage destination. Another interesting monument is **La Tour Brune**, a 12th-century tower which now contains a museum dedicated to the Écrins countryside (*Tel: (04) 92 43 49 48. Open: mid-Jun–mid-Sept Tue–Sat 10am–noon & 3–7pm, Sun 10am–noon*). Embrun's historically coveted geographical position now enables access to walking routes in the Parc National des Écrins, white-water rafting and canoeing on the Durance and an array of other sports. In winter, there is a small area of downhill slopes nearby at Les Orres. The **Office de Tourisme** (*Place Général Dosse. Tel: (04) 92 43 72 72. www.tourisme-embrun.com*) has all the information.

The picturesque snowy slopes of Montgenèvre

Tour: Lac de Serre-Ponçon

This tour is an introduction to the biggest man-made lake in Europe. Created between 1958 and 1962 to fulfil several practical purposes (hydroelectricity, irrigation and flood avoidance), Serre-Ponçon has become a photogenic holiday destination.

The route covers about 30km (19 miles) in one direction and driving time is about an hour to an hour and a half. Allow half a day with stops.

Start at the small town of Le Sauze-du-Lac, taking route D954 towards Savines-le-Lac.

1 Le Sauze-du-Lac

Nestling in the indented curve of the lake, this spot has views over both the Ubaye and Durance sections. In the centre of the village, as you drive in the direction of Savines, there is a left turn towards the lake, signed 'Belvédère' (lookout point), offering beautiful vistas.

Return from the lookout point to the main road and turn left. After about 3.5km (2 miles) there is a restaurant on the right followed by a car park with a sign for the 'Demoiselles Coiffées'.

2 Demoiselles Coiffées de Pontis

A 290m (317yd) stone-step path leads up to the top of this fascinating geological site, which consists of bizarrely shaped rock formations. As the 'Capped Maidens' are protected, visitors must keep to the path and cannot get too close.

Return to the D954 and turn left to continue approximately 7km (4½ miles) to Savines-le-Lac.

3 Savines-le-Lac

This small lakeside town has a sandy beach and offers watersports. Route N94 in the direction of Gap crosses the lake over the Pont de Savines. Although this is in the opposite direction to the continuation of the route, it is enjoyable just to drive across and back again for the views.

Take the N94 in the direction of Embrun and Briançon. After a couple of kilometres (just over a mile), take a right turn on to the D568 to the Abbaye de Boscodon.

4 Abbaye de Boscodon

Although inhabited by nuns, sections of the abbey are also open to the public (*Tel: (04) 92 43 14 45. Closed: Sun mornings*) and guided tours are offered on July and August afternoons.

It is possible to drive a little way into the forest that surrounds the abbey and there are also paths to explore on foot, including a short nature trail (ask at the abbey for details).

5 Forêt de Boscodon

This accessible forest contains a natural wealth of mountain trees.

Return to the N94 and continue to Embrun. At the approach to the town there are signs for a number of car parks outside the pedestrian central area. The Espace Delaroche and Parking du 19 Mars car parks are closest to the lookout point over the lake.

6 Embrun

This historic and pleasant town overlooks the lake from a rocky perch and makes a good base for exploration of the area. At the heart of the town is Place Barthelon, a pretty square with a fountain centrepiece and a bustling weekly market on Saturdays.

Head back out of town in the direction of Savines, but at the first roundabout take a right turn signed to the Plan d'Eau. There is on-street parking by the lake.

7 Le Plan d'Eau d'Embrun (Embrun Waterfront)

Embrun's waterfront area is a picturesque and tranquil spot. You can swim, rent a canoe or just stroll along the shore.

To return towards Savines and Le Sauze, take Avenue du Lac back to the N94 and turn right.

Tour: Lac de Serre-Ponçon

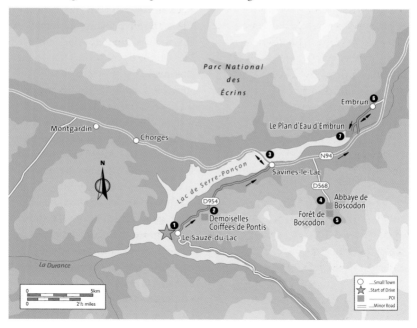

Gap

Although not a worthwhile holiday destination in its own right, Gap is the most sizeable town in the region and it is well located near the Parc National des Écrins and the Lac de Serre-Ponçon. The amiable town centre is especially animated on Saturdays, when a huge market fills the squares and lanes.

Parc National des Écrins

Two-thirds of the Écrins national park lies within Hautes-Alpes, with the other third in Isère. It preserves the wild natural beauty of the glacier-crowned Massif des Écrins and shelters many Alpine species. At the heart of the protected area is the towering 4,102m (13,458ft) Barre des Écrins summit.

Saturday market in Gap

SUNDIALS

One of the most charming architectural traditions of the southern Alps is the use of sundials to decorate buildings, taking advantage of the sunny climate. Many of the hundreds of dials still on show in the area today were made in the 18th and 19th centuries by travelling artists. They are particularly concentrated in towns and villages near the Italian border. Each sundial is unique and designs vary. Some are very simple, while others feature fresco paintings of natural themes, including the sun, the moon and birds, or more elaborate patterns. Moral mottos relating to the passage of time were also a popular adornment.

Paths in the core zone are restricted to pedestrians only, with cars and bikes banished to designated routes in the periphery. Information about the park can be acquired in Briançon, Embrun, Gap and Bourg d'Oisans or on the area website (*www.tourisme-oisans.com*).

La Grave

La Grave would be an obscure mountain village in the periphery of the Écrins had it not been adopted by the expert skiing and mountaineering community. Less experienced skiers are definitely better off elsewhere, as the slopes are mainly off-piste and difficult. In summer, the Glaciers de la Meije cable cars give access to a few hiking and mountain-biking trails, an ice cave and a stunning panoramic viewpoint. Details can be found at the **Office de Tourisme** (*Tel: (04) 76 79 90 05. www.lagrave-lameije.com & www.la-grave.com*).

Orcières

Much of the park's peripheral area consists of high valleys, woods, pastures and rustic villages such as Orcières, a starting point for rambling and hiking. Valley trails include gentle routes around other villages, hamlets, meadows and forested slopes. Higher and longer hikes can be accessed by cable car from the tiny nearby ski resort of Orcières-Merlette. Within half-day round-trip distance of the top of the cable car is a series of picturesque summit lakes. Routes are outlined at *www.orcieres.com*

Risoul

Fairly unknown internationally, probably because it is not close to any of the major airports, this quiet, relatively uncrowded ski resort is suited to families and those seeking a relaxing time. Links to the neighbouring resort of Vars create a sizeable ski area with attractive slopes mostly in the beginner and intermediate range.

Parc Naturel Régional du Queyras

The Queyras is a rural area next to the Italian border. Having been historically secluded, it retains a distinct cultural heritage. In 1977, the area was designated a regional natural park, with a view to promoting its charms to visitors and conserving the local wildlife. Today, there are marked hiking trails throughout the park. Traditional villages with visitor facilities include Saint-Véran, Abriès and Château-Queyras.

A buzzard circles above the wildlife-rich southern Alps

ALPES-DE-HAUTE-PROVENCE

Geological marvels, lavender fields, fruit trees and sleepy towns all nestle in the sunny valleys between the foothills of the Provençal Alps.

Dignes-les-Bains

The principal town of the Alpes-de-Haute-Provence, Dignes is surrounded by low mountains, but has a distinctly Provençal character. An eclectic mix of attractions brings visitors here, from the nearby geological reserve to the Tibetan museum. Lavender, which thrives in fields all around the town, takes centre stage at an annual late summer festival. Finally, there are the thermal waters that give Dignes its full name, which can be enjoyed at the **Établissement Thermal** (*Tel: (04) 92 32*

58 46. www.eurothermes.com. Open: Mar–early Dec. Admission charge).

Fondation Alexandra David-Néel

Alexandra David-Néel, a French writer and philosopher, made long voyages to Tibet and brought back a wealth of souvenirs, art and photographs, later leaving them to the town. The museum preserves her collections.

27 avenue Maréchal Juin. Tel: (04) 92 31 32 38. www.alexandra-david-neel.org. Open: year-round. Free admission.

Réserve Naturelle Géologique de Haute-Provence

This remarkable reserve consists of a number of scattered sites of geological interest. Among them are rock strata, ammonite fossils and extraordinarily well-preserved prehistoric bird footprints. The **Office de Tourisme** in Dignes-les-Bains (*Place du Tampinet. Tel: (04) 92 36 62 62. www.ot-digneslesbains.fr*) has guides and maps of the sites. More fossils, plus 3D models and contextual displays, can be seen at the reserve's informative museum, the **Musée-Promenade** (*Tel: (04) 92 36 70 70. www.resgeol04.org. Open: Jul–Aug 10am–12.30pm & 2–7pm; Sept–Jun 9am–noon & 2–4.30 or 5.30pm. Admission charge).*

Entrevaux

Historic Entrevaux is a peaceful southern town. The walled 11th-century town centre is accessed via a drawbridge and fortified gates. Even more distinctive is the citadel perched on a thin rocky hill above the town, connected to the town via a zigzag rampart. Along with the castle's battlements, this fascinating structure was the work of Vauban (*see p113*).

Vallée de l'Ubaye

The Ubaye valley borders the northern edge of the Mercantour and is fringed by rocky peaks. In the valley itself, meadows, scrublands, forests and orchards form a contrasting landscape. Amid the typical Alpine houses of the principal town, Barcelonette, are some extravagant villas built by returning locals who had emigrated to Mexico in the late 19th century and made their fortunes. Nearby, the small linked ski resorts of Pra Loup and La Foux d'Allox offer winter and summer sports.

Grand Canyon du Verdon

At the base of the Alpes-de-Haute-Provence, the extraordinary landscape of the Verdon canyon is protected by the Parc Naturel Régional du Verdon. The canyon consists of limestone cliffs split by a deep channel through which flows a surprisingly thin ribbon of a river. Moustiers-Sainte-Marie is the area's main town and a good base for visiting the park, with information provided at the **Maison du Parc** (*Tel: (04) 92 74 68 00. www.parcduverdon.fr*).

MERCANTOUR AREA

Despite being in close proximity to the Côte d'Azur, the Alpes-Maritimes mountains give the impression of being far from anywhere. This sense of remoteness stems from the fact that much of the area is protected within the Parc National du Mercantour (which also extends into Alpes-de-Haute-Provence). Even outside the park's core protected zone, the whole area is remarkably tranquil. With no major towns in the vicinity, all the visitor accommodation is in traditional villages or the occasional ski resort. Walking paths traverse the park, including sections of the long-distance hiking routes GR5 and GR52. Among the varied wild residents are wolves, several species of eagle (golden, short-toed and bearded), snow partridges, marmots and various hoofed animals (chamois, ibexes, moufflons and deer).

Vallée de la Tinée

As it meanders from the Col de la Bonette to its confluence with the river Var, the Tinée river passes through some truly spectacular landscapes. Parts of the valley lie within the Mercantour National Park's core zone and the rest is in its periphery. The D2205 road winds alongside the river round thickly forested hills and through dramatic gorges. A number of traditional hilltop villages are located near the route and these are the places to stay for exploring the Mercantour.

Auron

Auron is a charming village resort which looks magical in the snow. The village sits at 1,600m (5,250ft) and the highest point of the pistes is 2,450m

(*Cont. on p124*)

One of the many sundials that decorate the buildings in this region

Alpine geology

The complex geological processes that formed and moulded the Alps happened over millions of years, creating a mountain range with distinct areas and distinctive features. The original tectonic plate movements, the types of rock involved and the erosive actions of glaciers, rivers and the weather all played a part in creating the landscape. Dominating the complicated layout are the central massifs of Mont Blanc, Belledonne, Grandes Rousses, Écrins and the Mercantour. These high mountains are made of hard crystalline rocks and include numerous pointed 'needles' (aiguilles). With many peaks exceeding 3,000m (9,840ft), the Vanoise looms over the surrounding landscape like an extension of the central massifs. However, the rocks here are a mixture of crystalline and metamorphic, making the Vanoise part of an intra-Alpine zone that also comprises the Briançonnais and Queyras massifs and the upper Tarentaise and Maurienne valleys.

On the outer edges of the Alps are the Préalpes, including the massifs of the Bauges, Chartreuse, Vercors, Dévoluy and Digne. Mostly formed from softer limestone rocks, these foothill peaks were modelled into a variety of structures from rounded hills to steep cliffs and layered ridges. The Chablais is older than the other Préalpes and formed differently.

River valleys separate the massifs of the Préalpes from each other and also flow through the deep Alpine trench that divides the foothills from the central massifs. There are some remarkable gorges throughout the Préalpes, carved out by the paths of streams and rivers. Some of the most spectacular limestone gorges can be seen in the Chartreuse and the Vercors, as well as along the river Fier near Annecy. Meanwhile, in the southern Mercantour, the addition of another type of rock to the mix has led to a very different colour palette at another impressive gorge. From the upper Cians gorge to the middle Tinée valley around the village of Saint-Sauveur-sur-Tinée, the cliffs are made of red schist. These boldly coloured rocks lend a singular deep red hue to the landscape and create a striking contrast with the green of the trees. They are showcased especially well at the steep, narrow gorge where the Cians, more of a stream than a river, tumbles along its rocky path.

In places it almost seems like a touch of magic was applied in the formation of the Alps, given the wondrous shapes that some of the rocks are twisted into. One such site is the Demoiselles Coiffées ('Capped Maidens') near the Lac de Serre-Ponçon. Also described as Cheminées de Fées ('Fairies' Chimneys'), these are extraordinary columns of soft stony debris, which remain standing only because they are topped by protective pieces of more solid rock. Equally bizarre are the Rochers des Mées, a cluster of large upright stones rising above the village of Les Mées south of Sisteron. These rocks, too, have a poetic nickname: they are called Les Pénitents des Mées because they are said to resemble a bunch of penitent monks. Sisteron has its own dramatic rock feature in the form of the Rocher de la Baume, a towering exposed cliff face with deeply scored vertical strata. These are only some of the copious geological wonders scattered across the mountains.

Sisteron's eye-catching Rocher de la Baume

Auron village

(8,040ft). With mainly blue and red slopes, Auron is best suited to intermediate-level skiers and snowboarders. In summer, there are 12 trails of varying difficulty for walkers and mountain bikers.

Col de la Bonette

The Col de la Bonette is a high mountain pass connecting the Haute-Tinée valley with the Ubaye valley at the edge of the Mercantour area. At 2,860m (9,383ft) the Cime de la Bonette, reachable by a short uphill climb from the top of the pass, is one of the high summits of the park. There are excellent walking and marmot-spotting opportunities in the Vallon de Sestrière, near the Col de la Bonette, which can be reached from the tiny village of Saint-Dalmas-le-Selvage.

Isola and Isola 2000

Purpose-built Isola 2000 is the closest ski resort to Nice, only 88km (55 miles) from the airport. The ski area is roughly the same size as that of Auron, but because of the higher altitude it has a different aspect, with more exposed slopes. Isola has a good nursery zone for beginners and a decent selection of resort facilities. Most of the accommodation is in self-catering apartments. Italy is a manageable hike away, over the Col de la Lombarde.

Saint-Étienne-de-Tinée

The likeable town of Saint-Étienne is equipped with a **Maison du Parc** (*Tel: (04) 93 02 42 27. www.mercantour.eu, in French*), hotels, restaurants, shops and a lively marketplace. A number of walking trails start from here, and in the winter the town is linked to the Auron ski area.

Saint-Martin-Vésubie and Le Boréon

Saint-Martin-Vésubie has a decent collection of accommodation, shops and restaurants, plus an **Office de Tourisme** (*Tel: (04) 93 03 21 28. www.saintmartinvesubie.fr, in French*) and Maison du Parc (*Tel: (04) 93 03 23 15. www.mercantour.eu*) for information. A small road leads from the village up to Le Boréon, site of the Alpha wolf sanctuary (*see opposite*) and a gateway to the core zone of the Mercantour. There are some lovely woodland walking trails in this area, which can be accessed from a car park a little past the sanctuary.

Alpha

This large landscaped park is home to three packs of wolves, living semi-wild in large forested enclosures. Observation huts allow visitors to view the wolves from behind panes of glass. There is also a nature trail, informative exhibitions and a children's playground. *Tel: (04) 93 02 33 69. www.alpha-loup.com. Open: Jun–early Sept 10am–6pm (last admission 3.45pm); rest of the year, variable.*

Vallée des Merveilles

Hidden away in a particularly remote pocket of the Mercantour, the 'Valley of Wonders' is crammed with thousands of ancient stone carvings dating from the Bronze Age. Some of the engravings clearly depict objects such as tools and weapons. Others appear more symbolic and open to interpretation, from figures to concentric circles. The most celebrated engraving, known as 'le Sorcier' ('the Sorcerer'), is said to represent the primeval god Bego, namesake of Mont Bego, the peak that overlooks the site. Learn about the wonders, as well as the natural and pastoral history of the area, at the **Musée des Merveilles** (*Tende. Tel: (04) 93 04 32 50. www.museedes merveilles.com. Open: Jul–Sept daily 10am–6.30pm; May–Jun Wed–Mon 10am–6.30pm; mid-Oct–Apr (except closures during mid-Nov & mid-Mar) Wed–Mon 10am–5pm. Free admission*).

Valberg

Valberg is a medium-sized mountain resort with a family-oriented ambience in winter and summer. As a ski area it includes both downhill slopes and cross-country trails.

Unspoilt wilderness stretches for miles in the Mercantour

Protecting mountain species

One of the wonders of the Alps is the incredible ecodiversity found within this seemingly inhospitable environment. As the area has developed, protecting the many unique species that make their home here has become a key issue. A testament to the natural importance of the French Alps is that they contain three of the six national parks in mainland France: Les Écrins, Le Mercantour and La Vanoise. French national parks include core and partnership zones, which are governed differently. Core zones have extra protective status and a code of good practice limits the activities that are permitted within their boundaries to only those with the minimum environmental impact. In the partnership zones, the rules are less strict and are agreed by the local communities.

Achievements of the national parks include managing to reverse declines in numbers in several Alpine species. In 1963, when the Parc National de la Vanoise was set up, Alpine ibexes were critically endangered. Now these distinctive mountain goats are steadily making a comeback, with around 2,000 in the Vanoise and additional populations in the Écrins, the Mercantour and other remote areas. Another Alpine icon, the antelope-like chamois, has benefited significantly from conservation efforts in the Écrins and its numbers are estimated to have increased fivefold since the park's creation in 1973. Birds have also been a source of attention, with the Écrins placing golden eagles under special protection, and bearded vultures back in the skies through a re-introduction programme in the Mercantour.

The last of the three parks to be founded (in 1979), the Mercantour also became the only cross-border park when it was soon afterwards (in 1987) officially twinned with its Italian neighbour, the Parco Naturale delle Alpi Marittime. With a commitment to conservation on both sides of the border, Alpine species are able to cross freely between countries, which accounts for the spontaneous return of wolves to France. After disappearing for around 50 years, wolves were discovered to have made a natural return to the Mercantour when two were spotted there in 1992. Protecting them has proven to be a controversial move, sparking much debate between park conservationists and local sheep farmers. Alpha (*see p125*) outlines the conflicting views through animated exhibitions.

Other ecologically rich parts of the French Alps have been designated as regional natural parks. From north to south they are the Bauges, the Chartreuse, the Vercors, the Queyras and the Verdon. Each of these picturesque areas has distinctive landscape and ecosystem features, although there is also a lot of overlap of classic Alpine species. Residents of the regional parks include several species of owl (eagle, pygmy and Tengmalm's) in the Chartreuse, a thriving colony of bearded vultures in the Verdon and rare black salamanders in the Queyras.

All the parks also shelter varied species of plants, some of which are incredibly rare. The Mercantour, with its unique position at the crossroads of Alpine and Mediterranean environments, contains some exclusive species of plants that are not found anywhere else. Interesting flora of the high mountain parks includes the world's smallest tree, the dwarf willow, and the spiky, violet-coloured Alpine sea holly, which has protected status.

A protected wolf at a wildlife park in the Mercantour

Getting away from it all

Despite the popularity of the French Alps, there are many protected and remote areas offering quiet retreats. An alternative is to head north to the Jura mountain range, a little-known gem just on the other side of Lac Léman (Lake Geneva). For more variety, try the lavender-scented countryside of nearby Provence, the sun-soaked Mediterranean coast or an excursion into Italy or Switzerland.

National parks

Each of the Alpine national parks, the Écrins (*see p118*), the Vanoise (*see p75*) and the Mercantour (*see p120*), includes a central protected zone where civilisation is kept firmly at arm's length and the pace of life has to slow accordingly. With no cars or adrenalin sports disturbing the peace, these high-altitude landscapes feel wonderfully isolated and walkers are more likely to spot wildlife.

Remote rural areas

In between the liveliest towns and resorts of the Alps, there are whole valleys where tourism remains very low-key and traditional farming is still the main activity. The Beaufortain, southwest of Mont Blanc, is one such place, a rural idyll of forests, meadows and rounded mountains. The only roads in the area are small and meandering and pass through lovely villages. There are a few small-scale resorts, including Les Saisies and Arêches-Beaufort. One of the prettiest spots is the Barrage de Roselend, a turquoise artificial lake near Arêches. Other remote rural areas include the Massif des Bauges (*see p81*), a natural regional park containing nature trails and authentic villages, and the Vallée de la Clarée north of Briançon. Most of Provence and the Alpes-Maritimes also fall into this category.

The Jura

The Jura is a continuation of the Alps in both scenic and geographical terms, yet it receives far fewer visitors than its famous neighbour. This picturesque region has wide-ranging appeal, counting cross-country skiing, unspoilt pine forests and unique cuisine among its many attractions.

Arbois and Poligny

On the Jura gastronomic trail, pleasant Arbois is the place to try distinctive wines, including the unusual *vin jaune* (yellow wine). Walking and cycling trails weave around nearby vineyards and wine cellars; details can be found at the **Office de Tourisme** (*17 rue de l'Hôtel de Ville. Tel: 09 62 32 17 90. www.arbois.com*). Handsome medieval town Poligny is a partner of sorts to Arbois, famous for production of Comté cheeses, which you can pick up at a *fruitière* (cheese cooperative) as a perfect accompaniment to the wines.

Baume-les-Messieurs

Tiny Baume-les-Messieurs, an example of the pretty traditional villages dotted throughout the Jura, is surrounded by limestone cliffs containing some intriguing ancient caves full of stalactites and stalagmites. The **Grottes de Baume** (*Tel: (03) 84 48 23 02. Open: Apr–Sept 10am–5pm. Admission charge*), just south of the village, can be visited on guided tours.

Cascades du Hérisson

Although their popularity means they lack the characteristic Jura tranquillity and get crowded in summer, the seven waterfalls along the river Hérisson are stunning. A walking path leads past all of them in a three-hour round trip. *Tel: (03) 84 25 77 36. www.cascades-du-herisson.fr. Parking charge.*

Métabief Mont d'Or

At 1,463m (4,800ft), Mont d'Or ('Mountain of Gold') is the highest peak of the Jura, and Métabief is the main cross-country ski resort. Although the mountains here do not come close to matching the dizzying heights of the Alps, they get plenty of snow due to colder temperatures.

Barrage de Roselend in the peaceful Beaufortain area

Wildlife, such as this marmot, is easiest to spot in the national parks

Parc Naturel Régional du Haut-Jura

The remote Haut-Jura regional park is a mountain retreat of pine forests, lakes and plateaux. The Col de la Faucille boasts the most amazing roadside views. At the southeastern edge of the park is the compact ski resort of Mijoux. In summer, pedestrians can buy a return ticket to ascend to an altitude of 1,533m (5,030ft) via the Val Mijoux chairlift and Mont Rond cable car for an unrivalled view of Lac Léman and the Alps. On the northeastern fringe of the park and just a stone's throw from the Swiss border is the resort of Les Rousses. Most popular as a cross-country skiing area, it also offers some downhill skiing, plus assorted summer mountain sports. Activities can be arranged by the professional guide company **La Boîte à Montagne** (*Tel: (09) 50 24 39 34. www.laboitea montagne.fr*).

Côte d'Azur

Seaside excursions are a tempting addition to a mountain holiday. For especially stunning Mediterranean views, take a drive, a bus or a train along one of the *corniches* (coastal roads) from Nice. The Grande (Upper) Corniche threads a high panoramic path to Menton. The cliff-hugging Moyenne (Middle) Corniche stops at Monaco and is included in bus routes. Finally, the Corniche Inférieure (Lower) also goes all the way to Menton, tracing the curves of the seafront. A stretch of railway line, one of France's most scenic, follows the lower route.

Èze

Perched on a cliff about 12km (7½ miles) along the Moyenne Corniche from Nice, this medieval stone village is prettily secluded within ancient walls, with only one access gate. Once inside, the only way is up – past artisan boutiques, orange-tiled roofs and shady streets to the magnetically beautiful vistas from the top of the village. The interesting Jardin Exotique (*Open: 9am–sunset. Admission charge*), with its cacti and statues of goddesses, is a prime viewing spot. For a luxury night in this remarkable setting, check into the gorgeous **Château Eza** (*Rue de la Pise. Tel: (04) 93 41 12 24. www.chateau eza.com*). Staying in one of the ten very exclusive rooms at this former royal residence is definitely a special occasion option. Before they were grouped together as a castle 400 years ago, the stone buildings that make up the hotel were village houses, so each uniquely furnished room feels like a medieval hideaway. The gourmet restaurant and bar, which also feature spellbinding terrace views, are open to non-guests. Èze village is linked to the seaside resort of Èze-sur-Mer by the Chemin de Nietzsche, a steep path named after the 19th-century German philosopher, who found deep inspiration here.

Menton

The final point on the epic Route des Grandes Alpes, Menton is a restful sunny coastal town next to the Italian border.

Nice

Nice is a captivating city with a truly photogenic location, nestling between the crescent-shaped Baie des Anges ('Bay of Angels') and the Alpine

A mountain stream flowing from the Cascades du Hérisson

foothills. Although this is the glamorous Riviera, where sunbathing is practically as popular as eating (probably more so), Nice has a delightful character away from the beaches. To soak up its inimitable culture, history and atmosphere, make a beeline for the Old Town, where artists, markets, cafés and shops fill every space in the jumble of lanes and squares. Eating out in cosmopolitan Nice presents a challenge for the indecisive: it can be helpful to visit the **Office du Tourisme et des Congrès** (*5 promenade des Anglais. Tel: 0892 70 74 07. www.nicetourisme.com*) for listings. Two exceptional restaurants for special treats are **La Terrasse** (*Meridien, 1 promenade des Anglais. Tel: (04) 97 03 44 44. www.lemeridiennice.com. Open: Mar–Sept noon–10pm; Oct–Feb noon–4pm*) and the Michelin-starred **Aphrodite** (*10 boulevard Dubouchage. Tel: (04) 93 85 63 53. www.restaurant-aphrodite.com. Open: Tue–Sat*). La

Terrasse is an upmarket rooftop restaurant with an unrivalled view over the Baie des Anges. The food matches the sea breeze for freshness and includes high-quality versions of simple classics and amazing fruity desserts. The Aphrodite presents a gastronomic voyage of discovery steered by innovative chef David Faure, whose extraordinary style is evident in everything from the aperitifs to the desserts. The menu changes frequently, but is guaranteed to contain surprises (hint: dry ice and liquid nitrogen may feature!).

Provence

The famously beautiful countryside of Provence's sunny Vaucluse area, with its vivid lavender fields and lush vineyards, borders the Alps to the southwest. Avignon, the main city of the Vaucluse, will appeal to fans of art, architecture and culture. Provençal markets are as iconic as the scenery and can be found

The Côte d'Azur from the top of Èze village

The view towards Switzerland from Avoriaz

in most towns at weekends. Mont Ventoux (1,909m/6,263ft), as high as some of the mountains in the Alps but resolutely unique, has an exposed limestone summit, which appears from a distance to be covered in pale sand and beckons to a constant procession of ambitious cyclists.

Over the borders

With Italy and Switzerland within viewing distance from much of the French Alps, thoughts of cross-border excursions may well and justifiably spring to mind.

Italy

The Mont Blanc tunnel connects Chamonix to the ski resort of Courmayeur and the peaceful Aosta valley. Further south, there are several convenient points to cross into Italy's culturally distinctive Piedmont region. Routes to Turin via the town of Susa cross the border from the Maurienne valley and Montgenèvre. The latter is also part of the cross-border Voie Lactée/Via Lattea (Milky Way) network and a combined lift pass enables the novelty of skiing in Italian resorts.

Switzerland

One of the most relaxing ways to visit Switzerland is to take a leisurely boat trip across Lac Léman (Lake Geneva). The **Compagnie Générale de Navigation** (*Tel: +41 (0) 848 811 848. www.cgn.ch*) runs routes from Évian, Thonon and Yvoire to the other side of the lake, as well as longer cruises. Avoriaz (*see p104*) is just a few slopes from Switzerland, as is Vallorcine at the top of the Chamonix valley. It is easy to combine a trip to the French Alps with a day in Geneva, especially if you arrive and depart from there. A lovely big park lines much of the city's lakeside.

When to go

Most of the popular Alpine holiday activities are seasonal and the shape of tourism is completely transformed along with the scenery as the weather changes through the year. The busiest times are winter through to early spring, when snow is abundant, and the height of summer, when sunshine is. Late spring, early summer and autumn are considerably quieter and many resorts close at these times.

Climate

The weather in the mountains can vary significantly over a relatively small distance, due to the layout of the peaks and valleys, and can also change rapidly. Average temperatures are of little relevance in mountainous areas: checking forecasts daily is much more helpful. Temperature is broadly correlated to altitude, falling approximately 1°C for every 100m of climb (around 5°F for every 1,000ft).

Summers are warm, even hot in places, but with the aid of cable cars you can quickly go from a balmy valley resort to a chilly summit. The cooler northern Alps see abundant precipitation, although also significant amounts of sunshine, whereas the southern Alps are

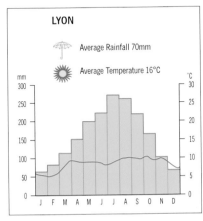

LYON

Average Rainfall 70mm

Average Temperature 16°C

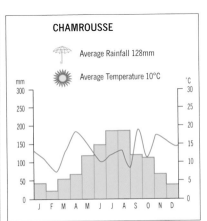

CHAMROUSSE

Average Rainfall 128mm

Average Temperature 10°C

WEATHER CONVERSION CHART

25.4mm = 1 inch

°F = 1.8 × °C + 32

drier and warmer, but with occasional heavy storms and the spring mistral wind of Provence. Weather in the Rhône valley is less dramatic. Forecasts are provided by **Météo France** (*Tel: 0836 68 02 followed by the 2-digit* département *code* (see p163). *www.meteofrance.com*).

Summer activities

July and August are the peak months for summer activities, when mountain resorts typically open some of their cable cars to allow walkers and cyclists access to the high peaks. The northern Alps are lush and green in summer, while the southern Alps are more Mediterranean. Most mountain resorts close between the main holiday seasons, so for visits outside these times it is advisable to stay in a town at lower altitude. Spring and autumn bring peace, quiet and beautiful landscapes, but the weather is more changeable and fewer activities are available. Many hotels have an annual autumn closure at some point, usually in November, and some also have a spring closure in May. Summer glacier skiing is offered at a couple of high-altitude resorts.

Winter activities

The winter sports season typically runs from mid-December to late April. Christmas, New Year and the French winter school holidays (in late February and early March) are the most expensive and busiest periods. Large groups of children in ski schools can create significant queues during the school holidays. January, early February and late March are good times to go, although January can be particularly cold and daylight hours are short. Cheaper breaks can also be had at the beginning and end of the season, but the snow is not as reliable in lower-altitude resorts at these times. The website *www.snow-forecast.com* gives a detailed forecast for all the ski resorts.

City and town breaks

French urbanites tend to take long holidays in August and head to the countryside or the coast. This means that the cities are quieter in August, but also that some small shops and restaurants close for much of the month. Spring, early summer and autumn are nice times of year to visit the cities of Lyon and Grenoble. The same goes for the most popular Alpine towns, notably Annecy, Chamonix and Briançon, which are significantly quieter outside high season.

Winter brings postcard-perfect snowy scenes

Getting around

Public transport systems and bike rental make it easy to get around towns and cities. Travelling between major destinations using regional train and bus networks is also fairly straightforward, but for getting around rural mountain areas it is best to have your own wheels. Driving in the French Alps presents significant challenges, so it is essential to be cautious and well prepared. However you travel, the spectacular scenery makes the journey part of the destination.

Public transport

The ease of getting around by public transport depends on how remote your destination is. Mountain resorts and natural parks can be difficult to get to, but public transport is being increasingly promoted and invested in, with incentives such as combined bus tickets and ski passes.

Access for travellers with disabilities

SNCF (*see below*) runs an information service advising on equipment, assistance and services available at stations (*Tel: 0890 64 06 50. www.accessibilite.sncf.fr, in French*). Many of the main regional stations are listed as *gares accessibles* (accessible stations), including Annecy, Bourg-Saint-Maurice, Grenoble and Lyon's major stations. Information is also available from station staff.

Buses, trams and metro

Lyon has a four-line metro and a four-line tram system (T1–T4). Single tickets and passes for two hours, one day or one evening can be bought from machines at metro stations or from tram or bus drivers. Grenoble has three tram lines (A–C), and tickets valid for trams and buses can be bought at tram stops or from bus drivers. Day passes are available at the transport (TAG) desks at the train station, in the **Maison du Tourisme** (*14 rue de la République. Tel: 0820 48 60 00*) and at the Grand'Place and Louis Maisonnat tram stops. Elsewhere, ask at tourist offices for information on local bus services – there are usually ticket kiosks in town centres. For all public transport, passengers are required to validate tickets before boarding. This involves inserting the ticket into a *composteur* (a small machine at the stop), which time-stamps it.

Regional train services

State-owned transport company **SNCF** (*www.sncf.fr*) operates almost all train services. Regional trains are called TER (Train Express Régional) and they run

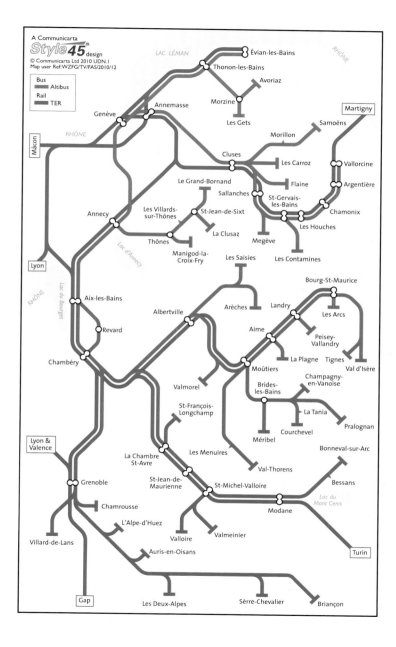

A Communicarta
Style45® design
© Communicarta Ltd 2010 UDN.1
Map user Ref:WZFG/TV/FAS/2010/12

Bus
  Altibus
Rail
  TER

LAC LÉMAN
RHÔNE
Évian-les-Bains
Thonon-les-Bains
Avoriaz
Annemasse
Morzine
Martigny
Genève
Samoëns
Les Gets
Morillon
RHÔNE
Mâcon
Cluses
Les Carroz
Vallorcine
Le Grand-Bornand
Flaine
Argentière
Sallanches
St-Gervais-
les-Bains
Les Villards-
sur-Thônes
St-Jean-de-Sixt
Chamonix
Annecy
La Clusaz
Les Houches
Thônes
Megève
Manigod-la-
Croix-Fry
Les Contamines
Lyon
Les Saisies
Loc d'Annecy
Bourg-St-Maurice
Aix-les-Bains
Arêches
Landry
Albertville
Les Arcs
Revard
Aime
Peisey-
Vallandry
Chambéry
La Plagne
Tignes
Moûtiers
Val d'Isère
Valmorel
Champagny-
en-Vanoise
Brides-
les-Bains
St-François-
Longchamp
La Tania
Courchevel
Pralognan
Méribel
Lyon &
Valence
Bonneval-sur-Arc
Les Menuires
La Chambre
St-Avre
Val-Thorens
Grenoble
St-Jean-de-
Maurienne
St-Michel-Valloire
Bessans
Chamrousse
Loc du
Mont Cenis
L'Alpe-d'Huez
Modane
Villard-de-Lans
Valloire
Valmeinier
Auris-en-Oisans
Gap
Les Deux-Alpes
Sèrre-Chevalier
Briançon
Turin
RHÔNE
Loc du Bourget

between major towns. There are almost always electronic machines as well as ticket desks at stations, and online bookings are also possible. At train stations, *composteurs* (validation machines) are yellow and located on or at the entrance to the platform.

Shuttles

Shuttle buses are a standard feature of ski resorts and are usually either free or covered by lift passes. They run between the lifts, resort centres and outlying areas. Timetables vary, but services into the evening are increasing.

Taxis and minibuses

Private bus companies operate shuttle services to some of the less accessible ski resorts. They include **Ben's Bus**, from Grenoble and Geneva airports (*www.bensbus.co.uk*), and **Actibus**, from Chambéry and Lyon airports plus some

TGV stations (*www.actibus.eu*). In towns, taxis tend to wait on the main squares or outside stations.

Driving

Driving is on the right, and at junctions priority is given to traffic from the right, unless road markings say otherwise. The speed limit in all inhabited areas (with place names) is 50km/h. Outside these areas the limit is 90km/h on N and D roads with no central divide, 110km/h on dual carriageways and 130km/h on *autoroutes* (motorways). In the rain, speed limits are reduced by 10km/h (20km/h on *autoroutes*), and speed is restricted to 50km/h on any roads affected by ice or snow, indicated by signs.

Road tolls

Motorway journeys generally involve paying a *péage* (toll) at some point. The amount varies depending on distance

A helicopter takes off from the altiport at Alpe d'Huez

and it can be paid in cash or with a credit card at the *péage* point.

Car hire and insurance
All the main European car rental companies have outlets in the region, at airports, train stations and town centres. International car rental broker **Car Hire 3000** (*Tel: 0800 44 73 30 00 (international freephone)/0800 358 7707 (from UK). www.carhire3000.com*) is a very useful contact. It has deals with most major companies and therefore offers some of the best available rates.

Safety and emergency breakdowns
Breakdown assistance should be provided through rental companies, but it is advisable to check the details and conditions. If bringing your own vehicle, ask your motoring organisation or insurance company about international cover. Note that French *autoroutes* are not covered by other breakdown schemes. Instead, there is a system of orange SOS phones every 2km (1¼ miles).

Cycling
Renting bikes is possible in every town and city. Outlets include Grenoble train station's **Métrovélo** (*Tel: 0820 22 38 38*) and Annecy's **Roul'ma poule** (*Tel: (04) 50 27 86 83. www.annecy-location-velo.com*). Lyon's self-service rental scheme, **Vélo'v** (*www.velov.grandlyon. com*), has been running successfully for years. The 340 stations around the city are equipped with cycle-route maps

Winding mountain passes connect the rural valleys

and credit-card machines for purchasing and recharging passes.

Flights
Although getting around the mountains by air is largely the preserve of the wealthy, visitors tempted by the prospect of bird's-eye mountain views may be interested in taking a short helicopter transfer. **SAF Hélicoptères** (*Winter: Héliport Courchevel 1850. Tel: (04) 79 08 00 91. Summer: Aérodrome Albertville-Tournon. Tel: (04) 79 38 48 29. www.saf-helicopters.com*) runs transfers between various French, Swiss and Italian resorts. A return journey between Les Deux Alpes and Alpe d'Huez, for example, costs €65.

Accommodation

Across the French Alps there is a diverse range of places to stay, from small rural guesthouses to ski chalets to urban hotels. Accommodation with highly original character can be found in every price bracket. There are often considerable differences in price between low and high season, and early booking is recommended for winter in ski resorts and summer in the most popular towns.

Hotels

The regional branches of the **French Government Tourist Office** (*see p168*) are good sources of information on hotels and other accommodation options. On their websites you can search by *département* or by town. Another useful organisation is **Logis de France** (*www.logishotels.com*), which represents fairly small independent hotels. Small hotels are often called *auberges* (inns), rather than *hôtels*.

Budget and mid-range hotels

All but the cheapest hotels have rooms with en-suite bathrooms and televisions as standard. Breakfast is always offered, but commonly costs extra on top of the room rates. Reception opening hours vary widely, with some smaller hotels shutting up shop quite early in the evening. Many independent hotels in the smaller towns and mountain resorts are family businesses and there is a lot of diversity between them in terms of organisation and ethos. The larger towns and cities also include some charming small hotels. Popular villages typically have at least one hotel, but in remote villages *chambres d'hôtes* (guesthouses) are usually the only choice (*see opposite*). There are many chain hotels in the region, and although these lack the character of independent hotels they can be convenient places to stay for a night. Chain hotels are often located on the main roads into towns, which is useful for visitors arriving by car. The **Accor** group (*www.accorhotels.com*), which runs Mercure, Ibis and other hotels, is the biggest chain.

Luxury and spa hotels

Besides top-end town hotels, the most luxurious places are often set in gorgeous renovated buildings, such as castles and huge farmhouses. In mountain resorts, many of the fanciest hotels have traditional chalet-style features, while others are emporiums of contemporary design. More unusual luxury options include staying in a tree-house (*see p185*). Spa facilities are often available in top-end hotels and are starting to become more widespread in mid-range places as well. The smallest spas typically consist of a jacuzzi and sauna, although many hotels also offer massage and other treatments.

Chambres d'hôtes and gîtes

These are family-run accommodations, usually in rural areas. *Chambres d'hôtes* are guest rooms in family homes on a B&B basis. Evening meals with the hosts (*tables d'hôtes*) are often offered at a surcharge. *Gîtes* are small self-catering apartments or cottages, usually annexed to the owner's home. The Paris-based organisation **Gîtes de France** is a useful source of listings (*Tel: (01) 49 70 75 75. www.gites-de-france.com*), as is the **French Government Tourist Office** (*see p168*).

Hostels, gîtes d'étape and refuges

There are two main *auberge de jeunesse* (youth hostel) associations in France: the **Fédération Unie des Auberges de Jeunesse** (*Tel: (01) 44 89 87 27. www.fuaj.org*) and the **Ligue Française pour les Auberges de Jeunesse** (*Tel: (01) 44 16 78 78. www.auberges-de-*

Le Royal hotel in Lyon

jeunesse.com). To stay in their hostels guests need to have a Hostelling International card, which costs €11 (under 26s) or €16 (over 26s) for a year. If you are spending just a few nights, it works out cheaper to ask for nightly 'welcome stamps'. *Gîtes d'étape* (stopover cottages) and *refuges* provide rustic, path-side mountain accommodation for hikers and other overnight adventurers. *Refuges* are the most remotely situated and are extremely basic, whereas stopover *gîtes* tend to be in or near villages on the routes and have more facilities. Both have dorm rooms and a place should be booked in advance. The **Club Alpin Français** (*www.cafresa.org*) has started an online reservation service for their refuges in the Mercantour and around Mont Blanc, which may be extended to cover other areas. Contact tourist offices for other listings.

Camping

The French Alps have a thriving summer camping scene and campsites are plentiful, especially in lakeside areas

Chambres d'hôtes allow a stay in the remotest villages

and in Chamonix. *Camping sauvage* (wild camping) is restricted to designated areas. In the national parks it is generally permitted as long as you are at least an hour's walk from the nearest road. Check with tourist or park offices for details. The official **French Government Tourist Offices** (*see p168*) and **Gîtes de France** (*see p141*) have campsite listings.

Ski accommodation

Accommodation in mountain resorts in the winter is very different from the rest of the year and the rest of the region. The seasonal price difference often transforms affordable summer hotels into expensive winter ones. Visitors on a budget typically opt for self-catering apartments, although package deals can bring down the cost of staying in chalets and hotels. Resort websites almost always include accommodation listings.

Chalets

Chalet accommodation is typically on a half-board weekly-booking basis, with evening meals served around a communal table, although some are self-catering and some offer shorter stays. They range from small enough (six to eight people) to be booked by a single group, to large chalet-hotels that rent each room separately. While some are quite simple, chalets in general tend to be more of a luxury option. Whirlpool baths are a fairly standard feature of the large chalets.

Self-catering apartments

Self-catering offers more flexibility than staying in a catered chalet and is a popular option in French resorts. The downside is that space often seems to be at a premium and apartments are traditionally advertised for as many people as they can possibly fit, including sofa beds in the living areas. For groups up for a crowded but cosy arrangement this can be a good way to bring down the substantial cost of skiing holidays. The self-catering market is widening, however, and there is now a reasonable choice of more spacious apartments in many resorts. Some of these are set in chalet-style buildings or converted farmhouses. Global holiday homes organisation **Interhome** (*www.interhome.co.uk*) carries a good selection of ski apartments in the French Alps.

Environmental consciousness

Upping their green credentials has become a positive trend in establishments across the accommodation categories. This is most evident in *eco-gîtes*, apartments, chalets and guesthouses that adhere to a set of environmentally sound principles such as using natural products, collecting rainwater and using renewable energy. *Gîtes panda* are a type of eco-gîte that has been further endorsed by the World Wildlife Fund (WWF) for their conservation commitment.

Food and drink

From the gastronomic delights of Lyon to the satisfying dishes of the mountains, the cuisine of the French Alps is distinctive and memorable. Plentiful local produce forms the basis for an array of regional specialities reflecting a tapestry of cultural influences. Meat, cheeses, fish, potatoes and mushrooms are staple ingredients, flavoured with Alpine or Provençal herbs and accompanied by regional wines.

Culinary culture

In the Alps, as throughout France, food is a major part of the culture. Meals are traditionally savoured over several courses, accompanied by bread and wine, although many people no longer have time for such long lunches. In contrast to lunch and dinner, breakfast is very simple – typically bread and jam with a coffee or hot chocolate and sometimes croissants or other pastries.

Regional specialities

Lyon

Bouchons, small bistro-type restaurants unique to Lyon, are ideal places to try out traditional specialities. One of the more adventurous of the numerous pork dishes on Lyon menus is *andouillette* (pigs' intestines sausage). *Salade Lyonnaise* has lettuce, croutons, *lardons* (bacon cubes) and poached egg. *Quenelles* are dumplings made with flour, cream and eggs, while *quenelles de brochet* are pike dumplings. *Fromage blanc* is popular, blended with garlic

and chives in *cervelle de canut* ('brain of the silk weaver') or served for dessert.

Grenoble and Isère

The best-known speciality of the old Dauphiné region is *gratin dauphinois*, a creamy layered baked dish made with sliced potatoes and milk. *Noix de Grenoble* (walnuts) pop up in many regional dishes.

Savoie and Haute-Savoie

Savoyard restaurants (as well as many in Isère) always offer the famous cheese feasts of fondue, raclette and tartiflette (*see 'Menu guide', p147*). Less well known is *farçon* (or *farcement*), a filling cake-like sweet and savoury blend of potatoes, bacon and dried fruits (typically prunes and raisins). Freshwater fish from Lac Léman makes a change to mountain cuisine.

Southern Alps

The Haute-Provence region has a distinctive cuisine. Herbs, olive oil and garlic are key ingredients. Specialities include *fougasse* (flat anchovy-topped bread) and *raïoles* (ravioli), typically stuffed with mushrooms or walnuts and served in a creamy sauce. Truffles are harvested in the south of the region.

Eating out

Restaurants usually propose a choice between set menus, with options for each course, and *à la carte* (choosing separate dishes from a varied menu). Set menus are almost universally cheaper than ordering from the *carte*, and lunch is cheaper than dinner. Besides standard restaurants, which open for lunch (usually between noon and 3pm) and dinner (between 7 and 9.30 or 10pm), there are several other types of eatery. Brasseries and bistros serve meals all day, while cafés serve snacks alongside coffee. The *salon de thé* (tearoom) is a chic variant on the traditional café. Rural *auberges* (inns) specialise in local food and provide accommodation. In cities and towns, *cafétérias* (self-service restaurants) and fast-food options are available. Finally, *glaceries* specialise in ice cream and *crêperies* in sweet and savoury crêpes. A service charge (12–15 per cent) is always included either in the menu prices or the total bill. Tipping is therefore not expected, although in restaurants many people do leave a small tip of a few euros.

The cosy interior of Restaurant l'Impossible, Chamonix

Self-catering
Markets
Food markets are a cultural institution throughout France, and wherever you are staying, you are sure to be near a good one. Fruit, vegetables, cheese, meat, fish and bread are all market staples and there are usually deli-type stalls offering ready-prepared snacks as well.

Specialist shops
Small local shops specialising in one type of produce can be found in every town and sizeable village. Smaller villages have *boulangeries* (bakeries) at the very least. Many places also have gourmet food shops, aimed at visitors and gift-shoppers, which sell a more varied selection of regional products.

Supermarkets
Big out-of-town supermarket brands include Carrefour and Géant. In city and town centres there are usually branches of Petit Casino.

Vegetarians
Vegetarianism is very rare in the French Alps and meat-free options are heavily cheese-focused, which can present a problem as many French cheeses are not vegetarian. However, dining out as a vegetarian is a manageable challenge. Vegetable pizzas are easy to find, as are large salads. Some restaurants even have an *assiette végétarienne* or *menu végétarien* (vegetarian dish or menu), although they are in the minority. Most hotels and restaurants should be able to

Fine, fresh produce is available everywhere

conjure something up specially. There are a few wholly vegetarian restaurants scattered about, and organic restaurants, enjoying a popularity surge, usually have a good range of veggie options. International restaurants can also be a good bet. Vegans will mainly have to rely on self-catering.

Drinks
Alcoholic

Wine (*vin*) always has been and probably always will be the dominant beverage of choice, but bars stock all the usual choices. Draught beer (*bière à la pression*) is served by the half pint (*demi*) as standard. *Apéritifs*, such as *kir* (white wine with cassis or fruit syrup), are commonly suggested before meals.

Vin chaud (mulled wine) is a winter staple. *Cidre* (cider) traditionally accompanies crêpes. Unusual local liqueurs include Chartreuse (*see p58*) and *liqueur de sapin* (fir-tree liqueur).

Non-alcoholic

Tap water is not only safe to drink, but also tastes good. Drinking fountains are commonplace. To order tap water in a restaurant, ask for *une carafe d'eau* (a jug of water). *Sirop* (fruit syrup diluted with water) features regularly on café menus. Coffee is extremely popular and usually served small and strong. For a large coffee, ask for *un grand café* (black) or *café au lait* (with milk). *Tisanes* (herbal teas) are more common than *thé noir* (regular black tea).

MENU GUIDE

Biologique (*bio*) – organic
Bifteck/entrecôte/faux filet – steak/rib-steak/sirloin
Charcuterie – cold, thinly sliced meats, usually sausages
Coquilles Saint-Jacques – scallops (often used in sauces)
Cuisses de grenouilles – frogs' legs (a speciality of La Dombes)
Fondue Bourguignonne – chunks of beef cooked at the table in hot oil
Fondue Savoyarde – melting pot of cheeses and white wine with bread cubes for dipping
Formule – two-course set menu
Galette – savoury wholemeal crêpe
Gâteau de Savoie – light sponge cake
Lardons – little cubes of bacon
Menu – three-course set menu
Poulet de Bresse – Bresse chicken (highly renowned)
Raclette – melting cheese poured over potatoes and accompanied by *charcuterie*
Saucisson chaud – chunks of sausage in sauce
Salade de chèvre chaud – warm goat's cheese salad
Tarte aux noix – walnut tart
Tartiflette – baked Reblochon (special Savoie cheese), potatoes, *crème fraîche*, *lardons* and onions
Tourton – pastry fritter stuffed with cheese or other ingredients

Entertainment

Entertainment in the French Alps really consists of two separate scenes: urban and après-ski. Lyon and Grenoble, as cities, have the most dynamic year-round nightlife. Smaller towns vary more with the seasons, becoming animated in the summer months, whereas mountain resorts have their liveliest evenings in the winter. Live music, festivals, cinemas and shows are among the most popular entertainment options.

Cities and towns

Le Petit Bulletin (*www.petit-bulletin.fr, in French*) publishes free weekly entertainment listings for Lyon and Grenoble and is distributed widely around each city. Grenoble also has the free weekly *Grenews*, available at the tourist office. Elsewhere, ask at town tourist offices for current listings.

Bars and pubs

In French culture, dinner is frequently an evening-filling affair, with diners enjoying pre- and after-dinner drinks as well as multiple-course meals. However, bars and pubs do have a place in the urban nightlife as well. Café terraces are perfect places for lingering on a warm summer evening and every town features them. Lyon's Place des Terreaux, Grenoble's Place Grenette and Chambéry's Place Saint-Léger are examples of big squares where you can watch the world go by over a drink. The Thiou canal supplies a romantic setting for evenings out in Annecy. Lyon also has a waterside nightlife along the east bank of the Rhône, an area known as Les Berges du Rhône, where a row of moored *péniches* (barges) is nightly transformed into twinkling bars and restaurants. Chamonix sees lively summer and winter nights, in the bars of the central area and the more bohemian Chamonix Sud district around the base of the Aiguille du Midi cable car. As well as cafés and bars, just about every sizeable town has English- or Irish-style pubs.

Cinema

Every town has at least one cinema and English-language films are frequently included in the programmes. Look for films that are listed as VO (*version originale*, with French subtitles), rather than VF (*version française*, dubbed). Cinemas favouring subtitling over dubbing include Lyon's **CNP Terreaux**, Grenoble's **Le Club** and **Cinéma Vox** in Chamonix (*see Directory listings*). Getting a chance to watch a film at the first-ever set, Le Hangar du Premier Film in Lyon (*see p171*), is a golden opportunity. Lyon's affiliation with cinema is further expressed every summer with showings on outdoor screens. For details, visit **Tout le Monde Dehors** ('Everybody Outside', *www.tlmd.lyon.fr, in French*), which also lists other outdoor entertainments, including concerts and games. Adult tickets typically cost around €7.50 in multiplexes and less in art-house cinemas. The website *www.allocine.fr* (in French) is a good general cinema listings search engine.

Live music

There are several popular live-music venues in Lyon and Grenoble. Principal jazz clubs are **Hot Club de Lyon** (*see Directory*) and **La Soupe au Choix** in Grenoble (*see Directory*). Concerts are held as part of festivals throughout the region and regularly at some venues such as **Le Transbordeur** (*3 boulevard Stalingrad. Tel: (04) 78 93 08 33. www.transbordeur.fr*) in outer Lyon and Grenoble's **MC2** (*see Directory*).

Nightclubs

Outside the ski season (*see p151*), opportunities to dance the night away are pretty much the preserve of Lyon and Grenoble, although Annecy and Chamonix have a few disco bars. Lyon's nightclubs attract a city-smart crowd, while in Grenoble the large student population definitely makes its presence felt.

Grenoble has a thriving pavement bar scene

Theatre, opera and dance

Fnac, a one-size-fits-all department store, also provides a ticket-booking and entertainment information service (*Tel: 0892 68 36 22. www.fnacspectacles.com, in French*). In the Lyon (*85 rue de la République*) and Grenoble (*4 rue Félix Poulet*) branches of Fnac, on-site ticket offices (*Open: Mon–Sat 10am–7pm*) cover shows at venues throughout the cities. **The Opéra de Lyon** (*see Directory*) is the region's main year-round classical venue. Lyon is also famous in the world of puppets, and traditional shows can be enjoyed at the **Théâtre La Maison de Guignol** (*see Directory*). In Grenoble, **MC2** (*see Directory*) also stages plays and dance performances. Aix-les-Bains has an open-air theatre for summer

Fireworks in Val d'Isère

performances and there are a few other small theatres in towns around the region.

Après-ski

In comparison with some other winter sports destinations of the world such as North America and Austria, France is not especially known for après-ski partying. Every resort has somewhere to relax with a drink after the lifts close, and most lay on family-friendly entertainments at some point, but only the liveliest places have a wider selection of bars and events.

Bars, pubs and nightclubs

At the foot of the main lifts in resort centres there is almost always at least one restaurant-bar where après-skiers soak up the last of the late afternoon sun on an outdoor terrace and order a *vin chaud* (mulled wine), *bière* or *chocolat chaud* (hot chocolate). In quieter resorts, designated bars are rare so evenings tend to be spent in restaurants or chalets. Resorts with a more energetic après-ski culture, such as Chamonix, Morzine and Méribel, usually have versions of the English or Irish pubs common to French towns, as well as trendier wine and cocktail bars. DJs and dance floors are fairly widespread in these livelier places and some have fully fledged nightclubs.

Events

Mountain resorts lay on public entertainments during the winter season. Some of these are regular features, while others are part of specific festivals. A classic fixture of the entertainment programme is the *descente à flambeau* (torchlit descent). These are organised by the ski schools and consist of processions of torch-carrying instructors and their newly competent students (frequently children) making their way down a piste in front of the resort centre. The timetable of torchlit descents varies from resort to resort and they are sometimes followed by firework displays. Live outdoor music, often jazz, is played in some resorts, such as Montgenèvre and Flaine. Christmas, New Year and the end of the season are universally celebrated with various festivities, such as concerts and fireworks. Val d'Isère is renowned for throwing one of the biggest end-of-season parties.

Night snow sports

As an unusual après-ski choice, try more skiing! More entertaining than sporty, illuminated after-dark skiing and sledging is offered by some resorts for the novelty value. Nocturnal skiing is usually only available on a couple of pistes on certain days. La Plagne's Olympic bobsleigh run and Morzine's Pleney sector are two of the places where thrill-seekers can put on a head-lamp and sledge down the night slopes. Ice rinks sometimes have late-night openings too.

Shopping

Although shopping is not one of the main activities that entice visitors to the Alps, it can be an enjoyable addition. Lyon offers extensive opportunities, while Grenoble and the towns have some interesting shopping areas on a smaller scale. Diverse independent shops have a strong presence in the historic town centres. Arts and crafts and delicious consumable treats such as chocolates and gourmet hampers are well represented.

Crafts and souvenirs

Traditional wooden crafts produced in the area included furniture, toys and religious statues. Wooden items are still sold in many shops today, although traditional production methods have mainly ceased. The earthenware tradition of Haute-Provence has been revived in some places. Many artists and artisans have set up small workshops and galleries in villages and towns throughout the Alps.

Lyon

There are numerous shops in the central streets between Place Bellecour and the Hôtel de Ville. Rue de la République is the most popular, but the roads running parallel to this main thoroughfare, such as Rue de Brest, are less busy and also lined with interesting outlets. A covered pedestrian street, Passage de l'Argue, features traditional shops as well as an affordable art gallery run by the cooperative **Carré d'Artistes** (*Tel: (04) 78 37 02 14.*

www.carredartistes.com). Other character-infused shopping areas are located in Croix Rousse and Vieux Lyon. True to the area's silk-weaving traditions, the retailers of Croix Rousse are mainly in the fashion industry, but other arts are represented as well. Montée de la Grande Côte and Passage Thiaffait are the best-known shopping streets. Vieux Lyon features a lot of crafts, decorative items, toys and edible gifts, particularly on and around Rue Saint-Jean and Rue du Boeuf. Opposite Part-Dieu station is a huge *centre commercial* (shopping centre).

Grenoble

In streets around Place Grenette interesting little shops entice browsers to pick up a souvenir or indulge a sweet tooth with some confectionery or chocolate. Grande-Rue, which leads off the square, has two brilliant bookshops: **Arthaud** and **Décitre**. High-street and boutique clothes shops line up around Place Victor Hugo. **Monoprix** (*22 rue*

Lafayette) is a useful one-stop shop for groceries, stationery, toiletries and various other items, with the added advantage of being open on Sunday mornings. Grenoble also has a large shopping centre, located at Grand'Place on tramline A.

Towns

Often pedestrianised and located in historic areas, main shopping streets in Alpine towns tend to be high in charm. In Annecy, the whole of the Old Town is dotted with appealing outlets stocking, among other things, jewellery, books, toys, chocolates, spices and gourmet foods. Rue Sainte-Claire is the busiest street, and quieter Rue Filaterie is also good. Briançon's Grande-Rue, in the middle of the Old Town, is the best street to wander in search of gifts, souvenirs and treats. In Évian-les-Bains, Rue Nationale is a hub of boutique shops. Chamonix, the place to go for serious mountain equipment, also has many other noteworthy shops.

Mountain resorts

Apart from a few resorts based on traditional villages (such as Val d'Isère), ski-resort shopping is generally limited to practicalities, plus the odd souvenir shop. Every ski resort has a shopping area featuring outlets for mountain clothes and sports equipment. Essentials such as sunblock are sold in pharmacies. There are usually a few food shops, always including bakeries and small supermarkets.

Local specialities tempt shoppers

Sport and leisure

*By far the biggest draw of the French Alps is the multitude of activities that turn the mountains into a year-round adventure playground. Summer is the season of variety, accommodating land, water and air-based sports. In winter, skiing and snowboarding take over, although there are also more unusual options. Tourist offices and resort websites provide comprehensive information to help visitors arrange their activities. **Anglo Info** (http://frenchalps.angloinfo.com) includes a directory of various sport and leisure companies.*

Summer

Aerial activities

Paragliding is extremely popular and companies all over the mountains propose tandem flights. Renowned areas include Chamonix, the Chartreuse and Lac d'Annecy. Some companies offer taster flights in hang-gliders, microlights and hot-air balloons. **The Fédération Française de Vol Libre** (*www.ffvl.fr, in French*) has listings of schools specialising in different types of unpowered flight.

Canyoning

Canyoning combines caving, swimming, diving and rock climbing into adventurous courses involving abseiling down waterfalls and following rivers through gorges. Courses are offered in many areas, including the Vercors, the Briançonnais and the Verdon canyon. **Club Alpin Français** has listings of professional guides and courses (*www.ffcam.fr, in French*).

Cycling and mountain biking

These sports have rocketed in popularity and designated routes traverse the mountains. The Portes du Soleil, Alpe d'Huez and Les Arcs are among the top resorts for mountain biking. Bikes and protective equipment are available for hire everywhere. See *www.mtbroutes.com/holidays* for listings of companies organising mountain-biking holidays. For cyclists, *www.grenoblecycling.com* lists all the Alpine cols (high-mountain passes) plus routes around Grenoble.

Fishing

Membership of a local angling club and a fishing permit are required under French law and various restrictions apply (*see www.unpf.fr, in French*).

Golf and tennis

Tennis courts are a standard facility and the mountainous backdrop makes for some truly scenic golf courses. **Golf Europe** lists many courses across the region (*www.golfeurope.com*).

Hiking and walking

Paths lace the mountain countryside, providing countless hiking opportunities. The longest routes are the *sentiers de grande randonnée* (GR, long-distance footpaths), which are numbered and designated by red-and-white-striped signs. GR5, from Lac Léman and Nice, is the most legendary Alpine hike. *www.gr-infos.com*

Horse riding

Riding centres located in many major resorts and towns offer lessons and tours. There are listings of clubs on the websites *www.equitation-rhonealpes.com* and *www.provence-equitation.com*

Mountaineering and rock climbing

Mont Blanc is the legendary mountaineering destination. The Écrins and Vanoise massifs are also used for expeditions. Rock climbing is practised across the region, as is *via ferrata*, a more accessible form of climbing using routes pre-fitted with handholds, rungs, cables and bridges. Qualified guides and training are essential for mountaineering and climbing. The **Club Alpin Français** (*www.ffcam.fr*) has contact details for local clubs.

Swimming

Léman, Annecy, Bourget, Aiguebelette and Serre-Ponçon lakes all have swimming beaches. Public pools, often with Jacuzzis and saunas, are found in most sizeable resorts. Male visitors may not be overjoyed to learn that a strict speedos-only dress code applies in all French public pools. Shorts are fine at beaches and at private hotel pools.

Watersports

Sailing, rowing and canoeing are widely available on the main lakes. Lac de Laffrey, near Grenoble, is ideal for learning windsurfing, which can also be tried on the bigger lakes. Waterskiing is available on Lac Léman. The

Paragliding over Lac d'Annecy

Hikers enjoy a tranquil path in the Portes du Soleil

Fédération Française de Voile (French Sailing Federation, *www.ffvoile.fr*) has listings of affiliated sailing clubs. Whitewater sports are practised on rivers and mountain streams. Rafting, done in a group on a large inflatable raft, is the simplest to learn; canoeing and kayaking require more time.

Winter

Ice-skating

The majority of mountain resorts have natural or artificial ice rinks, which are often free with lift passes.

Skiing and snowboarding

The *raison d'être* of many mountain resorts, downhill skiing and snowboarding in the French Alps have legions of devoted fans. Lift passes can typically be bought for anything from a half day to a week and can cover a single resort or linked area. Usually no lift pass is necessary to access the nursery slopes, learning areas for absolute beginners, generally located just above the resort centre. Every resort has rental shops for hiring skis, poles, boards and boots. Check your weight in kilograms, as ski bindings are adapted for weight. The **École du Ski Français** (ESF, *www.esf.net*) has instructors in every resort, but there are many other schools to choose from. Group lessons and private instruction are both widely available, but it is advisable to reserve in advance.

Many resorts have snow parks where skiers and snowboarders can practise their jumps and tricks.

For resort information and statistics geared towards snowboarders, visit *www.worldsnowboardguide.com*

Cross-country

Cross-country skiing is a way to enjoy the Alpine countryside at a slower pace, while getting plenty of exercise. Most ski resorts are equipped to offer some cross-country, with marked trails and equipment hire available. The Vercors (*www.vercors.com, in French*) and the Jura (*www.jura-tourism.com, see p128*) areas specialise in cross-country skiing.

Ski touring

Combining cross-country with sections of off-piste downhill, this is a sport for experienced skiers. Many mountain guides offer it as part of their repertoire. Ski touring packages can be booked through companies such as **Undiscovered Alps** (*www.undiscoveredalps.com*).

Sledding

Whizzing downhill in a bobsled or toboggan, possible in many resorts, offers an adrenalin rush without the physical exertion required by most winter sports. Some resorts arrange rides in sleds pulled by dogs. Clubs specialising in dog-sledding are listed on *www.chiens-de-traineau.com* (in French).

Snowshoe walking

One of the least technical snow sports, this is essentially hiking on snow with the aid of flat shoe attachments resembling tennis rackets. Snowshoes

are undergoing a renaissance in popularity due to the low environmental impact and rewarding experience of stepping lightly over snow. Guided tours are widely available and routes are outlined on local websites, such as that of Grenoble's **Maison de la Montagne** (*www.grenoble-montagne.com, in French*).

Other activities

Snowscooters (a cross between snowboards and scooters) and snowmobiles (mini motorbike-like vehicles) feature in some activity brochures. Ski joëring involves putting on skis and being pulled along by a horse. Ice climbing is the winter version of mountaineering, requiring serious equipment and training.

Skiers get ready at the top of a chairlift

Children

The mountain playground of the Alps is set up to welcome children as well as adults. Most of the sports described in the previous chapter are equally suited to young visitors. In addition, there are numerous activities aimed specifically at children and families, including adventure courses, pony rides and tourist trains. Simpler season-specific pleasures such as playing in the snow or swimming in a lake can also provide hours of fun.

Summer and year-round

Adventure parks

Numerous adventure parks tap into the potential of the region's forests with tree-top trails and obstacle courses. They include **Chamrousse Aventures** (*Tel: (04) 76 15 36 92. chamrousse-aventures.com*) near Grenoble; **Au Fil des Arbres** in Beaujolais (*Blacé. Tel: (04) 74 60 03 95. www.aufildesarbres.fr*); **Fourvière Aventures** in Lyon (*www.fourviere-aventures.com*); and **Indiana Park** in Morzine (*Tel: (04) 50 74 01 88. www.indianaaventures.com*). Timetables vary, but the parks are typically open daily in July and August, with reduced times the rest of the year.

Animals

Pony and donkey rides for children are widespread and a few companies, such as **Mont'Ânes** (*see p188*), also hire out donkeys to accompany families on hikes, carrying young children (or bags). Farm visits are arranged by some resorts, such as Les Gets. There are many wildlife parks, zoos and other attractions across the region, including the **Parc de Merlet**, near Chamonix (*see p86*) and **Touroparc**, a large zoo and leisure park 40km (25 miles) from Lyon (*Romanèche-Thorins. Tel: (03) 85 35 51 53. www.touroparc.com. Open: Jun–Aug 9.30am–7pm; Mar–May & Sept–early Nov 9am–5.30pm; Feb 10.30am–5.30pm. Admission charge*).

Mountain resorts

Most, if not all, resorts have play areas and organise activities for children. Outdoor swimming pools are often accompanied by paddling pools and water slides in family-focused complexes. Other facilities include miniature golf courses, trampolines and bouncy castles. Some resorts set up non-active entertainments such as puppet shows and crafts activities. Archery and paintballing are among the options that may interest older children.

Urban areas

Carousels, parks and playgrounds provide in-town entertainment. Pedalos may be hired on lakes in many locations, including Annecy and Lyon's Parc de la Tête d'Or. The latter also has specially designed carriages, a cross between pedalos and tricycles, for parents to pedal small children around the park. Lyon's puppet theatre, the **Théâtre La Maison de Guignol** (*see Directory*), has definite child-appeal.

Winter

Some ski resorts are more family-oriented than others: 'les p'tits Montagnards' is a logo carried by resorts that make particular efforts to welcome children. An example is Flaine, where the tourist office, tuning into the magnetic appeal of simply playing in the snow, arranges the annual 'Children's Reign', a week of free events in April such as snowman competitions and treasure hunts.

Children under five generally get free lift access. There are reduced ski-pass rates for older children, but the discount cut-off age varies and is often as young as 12 years. Many ski schools offer lessons especially for children.

Practicalities

Child-care centres, such as drop-in nurseries for under-fives, are available in many resorts. Older children can be enrolled in daily or weekly activity camps in some places. Tourist offices can often advise on babysitting services. Restaurants are usually accommodating to families with children. The main issue to bear in mind is that extra mountain safety and health precautions must be taken for children. Those under three years old should not go to altitudes above 2,000m (6,560ft) and it is advisable to keep under-12s from spending too much time above 2,500m (8,200ft).

The children's playground at Tignes

Essentials

Arriving and departing

By air

Lyon-Saint Exupéry
(*www.lyonaeroports.com*) and Geneva
(*www.gva.ch*) airports are the region's
main hubs. Flights to Grenoble
(*www.grenoble-airport.com*) and
Chambéry (*www.chambery-
airport.com*) increase in the peak
season. Nice (*www.nice.aeroport.fr*) and
Turin (*www.aeroportoditorino.it*)
airports are useful for some parts of the
French Alps. Airlines with flights to and
from all these airports are listed on
www.skyscanner.net

By rail

Travelling by rail is a pleasant
alternative to flying, with speedy TGV
trains crossing France in no time.
Eurostar (*Tel: bookings: +44 (0) 8432
186 186. www.eurostar.com*) can book
the whole route: London to Lyon takes
about six hours and London to
Grenoble six and a half, including Paris
connection time. Another useful
website for routes and tickets is
www.raileurope.co.uk

By road

It is feasible to drive to the Alps from
Paris or Calais. Lyon from Paris
generally takes about four and a half
hours, and from Calais approximately
seven hours; add an extra hour for
Grenoble. To drive to remote ski
resorts, such as Val d'Isère, allow several
hours from Grenoble.

Customs

Duty-free limits apply to travellers
bringing goods into France from non-
EU countries and only travellers leaving
the EU can take advantage of duty-free
shopping. For detailed information, see
the website *www.douane.gouv.fr*

Electricity

France uses the continental two-round-
pin plug system, with an electric
current of 220 volts.

Internet

Most hotels have Internet connection in
the rooms, which may be free or
charged. Wi-Fi access is increasingly
available at tourist offices, cafés and bars,
and town centres have Internet cafés.

THE SKI TRAIN

Every weekend from mid-December to mid-
April, Eurostar operates a special direct
service between the UK and the Alps. Trains
from London St Pancras and Ashford stop
only in Lille before continuing to Moûtiers,
Aime la Plagne and Bourg-Saint-Maurice.
Passengers hopping on a train on a Friday
evening (overnight service), Saturday or
Sunday morning emerge in the mountains
seven to eight hours later, having made a
carbon-neutral journey with minimum effort.
Tickets start at £84 single, £149 return, and
'ski deals' offer savings on accommodation
and travel booked together.

Money

France uses the euro. ATMs (*points d'argent*, or cash points) represent an easy way to manage money. Paying for items and services by credit and debit cards with a chip and PIN is usually possible, but not always, so take cash with you into more remote areas.

Opening hours

Opening hours frequently change with the seasons. In general, shops open Monday to Saturday from about 9am to 7 or 8pm, but lunchtime closures are commonplace. Resort tourist offices open similar hours in high season. Due to government regulations, almost every shop is shut on Sundays, although those selling food or aimed at tourists are allowed to open and some do. Many attractions open on Sundays but close on a weekday, usually Monday or Tuesday, sometimes Wednesday. Banks keep particularly inconsistent hours; mornings are most reliable.

Passports and visas

EU nationals do not need a visa and only require a passport valid for their stay in France. All other visitors must have passports valid for at least three months from the date of arrival for short tourist stays (more for business or longer trips). Short stays (under 90 days) without a visa are allowed for citizens of certain countries, including Australia, Canada, New Zealand and the USA. Other visitors need to apply

CONVERSION TABLE

FROM	TO	MULTIPLY BY
Inches	Centimetres	2.54
Feet	Metres	0.3048
Yards	Metres	0.9144
Miles	Kilometres	1.6090
Acres	Hectares	0.4047
Gallons	Litres	4.5460
Ounces	Grams	28.35
Pounds	Grams	453.6
Pounds	Kilograms	0.4536
Tons	Tonnes	1.0160

To convert back, for example, from centimetres to inches, divide by the number in the third column.

MEN'S SUITS

UK	36	38	40	42	44	46	48
Rest of Europe	46	48	50	52	54	56	58
USA	36	38	40	42	44	46	48

DRESS SIZES

UK	8	10	12	14	16	18
France	36	38	40	42	44	46
Italy	38	40	42	44	46	48
Rest of Europe	34	36	38	40	42	44
USA	6	8	10	12	14	16

MEN'S SHIRTS

UK	14	14.5	15	15.5	16	16.5	17
Rest of Europe	36	37	38	39/40	41	42	43
USA	14	14.5	15	15.5	16	16.5	17

MEN'S SHOES

UK	7	7.5	8.5	9.5	10.5	11
Rest of Europe	41	42	43	44	45	46
USA	8	8.5	9.5	10.5	11.5	12

WOMEN'S SHOES

UK	4.5	5	5.5	6	6.5	7
Rest of Europe	38	38	39	39	40	41
USA	6	6.5	7	7.5	8	8.5

for a Schengen visa, permitting 90 days of unlimited travel in France and 14 other EU countries. See *www.diplomatie.gouv.fr* for details.

Pharmacies

Pharmacies are easy to spot due to the large flashing green cross outside. Typical timetables are Monday to Saturday 9am to 7 or 8pm. A rota system overnight and on Sundays ensures there is an open pharmacy in the vicinity.

Post

Post offices are typically open Monday to Friday (with a break for lunch) and Saturday mornings. Stamps (*timbres*) are also sold at *tabacs* and newsagents.

Public holidays

France has 13 public holidays:
1 January – Jour de l'An (New Year's Day)
March/April – Pâques (Easter Sunday and Monday)
1 May – Fête du Travail (May Day/ Labour Day)
8 May – Victoire 1945 (VE Day)
40th day after Easter – L'Ascension (Ascension Thursday)
7th Sunday after Easter – Pentecôte (Whit Sunday and Monday)
14 July – Fête Nationale (Bastille Day)
15 August – L'Assomption (Assumption)
1 November – La Toussaint (All Saints' Day)
11 November – Jour d'Armistice (Remembrance Day)
25 December – Noël (Christmas Day)

Smoking

Smoking is banned in all indoor public venues, including restaurants and bars, but it is permitted on terraces.

Suggested reading and media
Books

Bocuse in Your Kitchen: Simple French Recipes for the Home Chef, Paul Bocuse (Flammarion).
Mountain Biking Europe, Chris Moran and Rowan Sorrell (Footprint) – features the best-known Alpine resorts.
The Alps: A Bird's Eye View, Janez Bizjak and Matevz Lenarcic (Pan Alp) – stunning aerial photographs and some text.
The GR5 Trail Through the French Alps: Lake Geneva to Nice, Paddy Dillon (Cicerone Press) – details the famous hiking route.
Where to Ski and Snowboard, Chris Gill and Dave Watts (NortonWood Publishing) – international ski resort guide, updated yearly.

Films

The Horseman on the Roof (1995) by director Jean-Paul Rappeneau – a period film shot in the French Alps, which won a César award for cinematography.
The World is Not Enough (1999) by director Michael Apted – James Bond drops from a helicopter and skis down Mont Blanc.

Tax

A *taxe de séjour*, of €0.9 per person per day, is charged at every accommodation. Visitors from non-EU countries can claim a VAT rebate on some expensive single purchases. Ask in stores for details.

Telephones

The country code for France is 33. Telephone numbers throughout southeast France start with 04, followed by a two-digit *département* code. Mobile numbers start with 06. Numbers beginning 0800, 0804, 0805 or 0809 are free to call from landlines; charges vary for other 08 numbers. Payphones, available in every town, require phonecards, sold in *tabacs*.

Département codes
Ain – *01*
Alpes-de-Haute-Provence – *04*
Alpes-Maritimes – *06*
Drôme – *26*
Hautes-Alpes – *05*
Haute-Savoie – *74*
Isère – *38*
Rhône – *69*
Savoie – *73*

Time

The time zone in France is GMT+1 hour. The 24-hour clock is used instead of am and pm.

Toilets

Public toilets are available at all visitor attractions, in ski stations and town centres and by motorways. They are generally free, except at train stations.

Pharmacies are available in every town centre

Travellers with disabilities

Steep inclines and narrow cobbled streets can pose major difficulties. Tourist office brochures designate wheelchair-accessible sites and France's **'Tourisme & Handicaps'** label (*www.tourisme-handicaps.org*) is awarded to attractions and establishments meeting accessibility criteria in one or more of the categories of physical, mental, visual and hearing disabilities. Travellers with disabilities receive discounted rates at some attractions. **L'École du Ski Français** (*www.esf.net*) lists resorts offering Handiski, specialist equipment and guides for skiers with physical disabilities and visual impairments.

Language

Basic French phrases and pronunciation
In French the letter 'j' corresponds to the 's' sound in words like 'leisure' and 'measure' (written here as 'zh'). Letters 'n' and 'm' at the end of syllables are not pronounced, but give preceding vowels a nasal sound.

English	French	Pronunciation
Hello	Bonjour	bon-zhoor
Good evening	Bon soir	bon-swuh
Goodbye	Au revoir	o-rer-vwa
Please	S'il vous plait	seel voo play
Thank you (very much)	Merci (beaucoup)	mair-see (bow-coo)
You're welcome	Je vous en prie	zher voo-zon pree
You're welcome (inf)	De rien	der ree-en
Excuse me	Excusez-moi	Ek-skew-zay-mwa
Sorry (forgive me)	Pardon	par-don
Do you speak English?	Parlez-vous anglais?	Par-lay-voo-onglay
I'm looking for...	Je cherche...	zher shershe
Where is...?	Où est...?	oo-ay
I'd like...	Je voudrais...	je voo-dray
How much is it?	C'est combien?	say kom-byun
I'm lost	Je me suis égaré(e) (m/f)	zher mer swee-zay-garay
Can you show me on the map?	Pouvez-vous m'indiquer sur la carte?	poo-vay-voo mun-dee-kay sewr la kart
Go straight ahead	Continuez tout droit	kon-teen-way too dwa
Turn left/right	Tournez à gauche/droite	toor-nay a gohsh / dwut

Specific vocabulary

English	French
Mountaineering	Alpinisme (m)
Panoramic viewpoint	Belvédère (m)
Ticket office	Billeterie (f)
Guide agency	Bureau (m) des guides
Fishing permit	Carte (f) de pêche
Give way	Cédez la priorité
Mogul field (bumps on piste)	Champ (m) de bosse

English	French
Mountain pass	Col (m)
Cycling	Cyclisme (m)
Tasting	Dégustation (f)
Hang-gliding	Deltaplane (m)
White water	Eau (f) vive
Horse riding	Équitation (f)
Climbing	Escalade (f)
Petrol station	Poste (m) d'essence/Station-service (f)
(Lift) pass	Forfait (m) (skieur)
Funicular (railway)	Funiculaire (m)
Public holiday	Jour férié (m)
Headquarters/Visitor centre of park	Maison du parc (f)
Information centre for mountain activities	Maison (f) de la montagne
Hot-air balloon	Montgolfière (f)
Shuttle bus, boat or train	Navette (f)
Paragliding	Parapente (m)
Toll	Péage (m)
Weather forecast	Prévisions (fpl) météo
Slow down	Ralentissez
Hike	Randonnée (f, short: rando)
Snowshoes	Raquettes (fpl)
Ski lifts	Remontées mécaniques (fpl)
Trail	Sentier (m)
Nature trail	Sentier de découverte
Downhill skiing	Ski (m) alpin/de piste
Cross-country skiing	Ski nordique/ski de fond
Exit	Sortie (f)
Snowboarding	Surf (m) des neiges
Viewpoint indicator	Table d'orientation (f)
Gondola	Télécabine (f)
Cable car	Téléphérique (m)
Chairlift	Télésiège (m)
Drag lift	Téléski (m)
Black ice (on road)	Verglas (m)
Sailing	Voile (f)
Microlight flight	Vol (m) ULM
Mountain biking	VTT; vélo tout terrain

Emergencies

Emergency numbers
All emergencies: *112*
Ambulance (SAMU): *15*
Fire (Pompiers): *18*
Police: *17*

Health risks
Always be prepared for sudden changes in mountain temperature and weather. Carry layers of clothing, waterproofs and plenty of water. There is a heightened risk of sunburn in the mountains, which should not be underestimated in summer and winter equally. Altitude sickness is caused by a lack of oxygen in people who have not yet acclimatised to the change in atmospheric pressure. It is most common above 3,000m (9,840ft), although it can have an effect from 2,500m (8,200ft). Mild symptoms (which include headache, dizziness and loss of appetite) can be treated with rest and medications if necessary. Medical attention should be sought immediately for any serious symptoms as altitude sickness can be dangerous in rare cases.

Insurance
Generic travel insurance schemes are not all-encompassing enough to cover eventualities such as mountain rescues. In ski resorts, the easiest option is to add insurance when buying your lift pass. All resorts offer this for a minimal sum (€2.50 per day). The scheme,

Carré Neige (*www.carreneige.com*), includes emergency rescue, medical and transport costs.

Medical services
Pharmacies are the first port of call for minor ailments. For more specialist healthcare, visit a hospital casualty department (*salle des urgences*) or doctor's surgery (*cabinet de médecin*). Pharmacists and tourist offices can advise on where the nearest one is. EU citizens should carry the European Health Insurance Card (EHIC, *www.ehic.org.uk*), which covers emergency medical treatment and enables partial reimbursement of other costs. Non-EU visitors have to pay for all treatment and seek a refund from their insurance providers. Dentists and opticians are widely available.

Police
Police officers wear a dark blue uniform and drive dark blue cars. They are entitled to stop anyone and ask for ID. If you need a police station, ask for *la gendarmerie* or *la police municipale*.

Safety and crime
Mountain safety hinges on being sensible, prepared and informed. Respect the limits of your experience level in any adventurous sport, seek advice and training where needed, and always heed weather and avalanche

warnings (*see p72*). Ski helmets, which children should certainly wear and adults may choose to wear, are available at rental shops.

Visitors to mountain resorts are unlikely to be victims of any crimes. Most people leave skis unattended without concern, but locks are available for peace of mind. In urban areas, car crime is an issue, but the risk can be substantially reduced by never leaving anything at all in parked cars. Pickpocketing can also be a problem in the cities, so take sensible precautions.

Embassies and consulates

Although all foreign embassies are located in Paris, some countries have consulates in southern France. The closest embassy or consulate to the Alps is listed in each case.

Australia – Paris Embassy
4 rue Jean Rey, 15e. Tel: (01) 40 59 33 00. www.france.embassy.gov.au

Canada – Paris Embassy
35 avenue Montaigne. Tel: (01) 44 43 29 00. www.canadainternational.gc.ca/france

New Zealand – Paris Embassy
7 rue Léonard de Vinci, 16e. Tel: (01) 45 01 43 43. www.nzembassy.com/france

South Africa – Paris Embassy
59 quai d'Orsay, 7e. Tel: (01) 53 59 23 23. www.afriquesud.net

UK – Lyon Consulate
24 rue Childebert. Tel: (04) 72 77 81 70. ukinfrance.fco.gov.uk

USA – Lyon Consulate
1 quai Jules Courmont. Tel: (04) 78 38 36 88. france.usembassy.gov

Specialist safety equipment is required for mountaineering

Directory

Accommodation price guide

This price guide is based on a standard double room for one night, without any meals unless otherwise stated. As tariffs in ski resorts vary wildly across low, medium and high seasons, the price brackets for each establishment are based on the medium season. If summer and winter are very different, two categories are included.

£	less than €60
££	€60–110
£££	€110–180
££££	more than €180

Eating out price guide

This price guide is based on an average-priced set menu (*menu* or *formule*), or two courses where there is no set menu, without drinks. Restaurants are open daily for lunch and dinner unless otherwise stated.

£	less than €15
££	€15–30
£££	€30–50
££££	more than €50

Information

For useful regional information and advice, contact the relevant branches of the French Government Tourist Office:

Rhône-Alpes Tourisme
8 rue Paul Montrochet, Lyon. Tel: (04) 26 73 31 59. www.rhonealpes-tourisme.com

Savoie-Mont-Blanc Tourisme
24 boulevard de la Colonne, Chambéry, & 20 avenue du Parmelan, Annecy. Tel: 0820 00 73 74. www.savoie-mont-blanc.com

Provence-Alpes-Côte d'Azur Tourisme
Maison de la Région, 61 La Canebière, Marseille. Tel: (04) 91 56 47 00. www.decouverte-paca.fr

LYON AND THE RHÔNE VALLEY

Vieux Lyon

ACCOMMODATION

College Hotel £££
Amazingly bright white rooms with outdoor seating on cute balconies serve as a curious contrast to the wooden furniture and laden bookcases of the dining area which is decked out like an old-school library.
5 place Saint-Paul. Tel: (04) 72 10 05 05. www.college-hotel.com

EATING OUT

Le Banana's £
Serving ice creams, café meals, drinks and, most importantly, a varied selection of delicious sweet or savoury crêpes, best paired with a jug of cider.
1 place du Gouvernement. Tel: (04) 72 40 94 98.

Nardone £
Rightly famed for amazing ice cream, which comes in a dazzling array of flavours, this riverside

café also does crêpes and other sweet treats.
26 quai de Bondy.
www.glaciernardone.com.
Open: summer Mon–Sun 9am–1am; winter Wed–Sun 10am–7pm.

Le Tire Bouchon ££
A charming bistro, 'The Corkscrew' provides meals of both quality and quantity at reasonable prices.
16 rue du Bœuf. Tel: (04) 78 37 69 95. Open: Tue–Sat 7.30–10pm.

Les Adrets ££–£££
Good-quality hearty traditional Lyon food is complemented by the warm, rustic, wooden-beam style of this inviting restaurant.
30 rue du Bœuf.
Tel: (04) 78 38 24 30.
Closed: August.

ENTERTAINMENT
Smoking Dog
The daytime café culture of Vieux Lyon merges seamlessly into evening bar culture. This English-style pub is one of the most popular destinations.
16 rue Lainerie. Tel: (04) 78 28 38 27. Open: Mon–Fri 5pm–1am, Sat–Sun 2pm–1am.

Théâtre La Maison de Guignol
Traditional puppet theatre, with family-friendly shows on Wednesdays and weekends, plus extra holiday performances, and Friday evening dinner shows for adults. Booking essential.
2 montée du Gourguillon, Saint-Georges.
Tel: (04) 72 40 26 61.
www.lamaisondeguignol.fr

Presqu'île and Croix Rousse
ACCOMMODATION
Hotel de la Marne ££
This welcoming hotel provides great value for a central Lyon base. The staff are friendly and helpful. A generous breakfast is included, along with free Wi-Fi.
78 rue de la Charité.
Tel: (04) 78 37 07 46.
www.hoteldelamarne.fr

B4 Lyon Grand Hotel £££
Well located in the Presqu'île, this is a classic, elegant hotel with spacious rooms filled with light from tall windows. Huge bathrooms and lounge areas in the

bedrooms add to the sense of luxury.
11 rue Grolée.
Tel: (04) 72 40 45 45.
www.boscolohotels.com

Le Royal ££££
Originally opened in 1912 and recently refurbished by renowned architects and designers, the standout features of this grand central establishment include luxurious textiles. The dining room is an ultra-stylish version of a French country home kitchen, while the bar has velvet tapestries, displays of silk bobbins and a jazz and blues soundtrack.
20 place Bellecour.
Tel: (04) 72 41 64 41.
lyonhotel-leroyal.com

EATING OUT
Toutes les Couleurs £–££
At this bohemian organic vegetarian restaurant, vegan and gluten-free options are also available.
26 rue Imbert Colomès.
Tel: (04) 72 00 03 95.
www.touteslescouleurs.fr.
Open: Tue–Sat lunch, Fri–Sat dinner. Closed: Aug (specific dates vary).

Café du Gros Caillou ££

With outdoor seating on the edge of Croix Rousse hill, there is a great view from here both day and night.

180 boulevard de la Croix-Rousse.
Tel: (04) 78 27 22 37.

Les Garçons Chasseurs ££

An eclectic menu with dishes from around the world. The focus is on unusual meats, such as crocodile and gnu.

20 rue Terme. Tel: (04) 78 91 09 01. www. lesgarconschasseurs.com. Open: Tue–Sat noon–late evening.

Magali et Martin ££

A modern take on the traditional *bouchon* (Lyonnais bistro), with imaginative creations that change according to seasonal ingredients found in local food markets. Bookings are essential.

11 rue Augustins. Tel: (04) 72 00 88 01.

Le Sud ££

With the idea of democratising fine cuisine, legendary chef Paul Bocuse opened this and four other brasseries (L'Ouest, Le Nord, L'Est and Argenson). The theme of Le Sud is 'sunshine', with a menu full of colourful Mediterranean fare.

11 place Antonin-Poncet. www.nordsudbrasseries. com. Tel: (04) 72 77 80 00.

Le Comptoir des Marronniers ££–£££

Situated on the avenue of gastronomy that is Rue des Marronniers, this place is at the top of the street in location and quality, featuring gourmet Lyonnais specialities.

8 rue des Marronniers. Tel: (04) 72 77 10 00.

ENTERTAINMENT

CNP Terreaux

Cinema showing original-language versions of international films.

40 rue du Président Edouard Herriot. Tel: 0892 68 69 33.

Hot Club de Lyon

Lyon's number one live jazz venue.

26 rue de la Lanterne. Tel: (04) 78 39 54 74. www.hotclubjazz.com (in French).

Opéra de Lyon

The selection of opera and dance performances and concerts (classical, world music and jazz) at Lyon's most classic venue includes special family shows.

Place de la Comédie. Tel: 0826 30 53 25. www.opera-lyon.com

Soda Bar

Cocktails both classic and innovative are mixed – and sometimes set alight – by the bottle-juggling staff, with DJ sets on Thursdays, Fridays and Saturdays.

7 rue de la Matinière. Open: Mon–Sat 6pm–3am.

Part-Dieu and Rive Gauche

ACCOMMODATION

Park & Suites Prestige Lyon Part-Dieu ££–£££

Combining hotel services (including breakfast) with the flexibility of self-catering accommodation, this smart and comfortable apart-hotel provides the best of both worlds. Park & Suites also have several other self-catering properties in Lyon and across the region to suit a range of budgets.

111 boulevard Marius

Vivier Merle.
Tel: (04) 72 84 10 40.
www.parkandsuites.com

EATING OUT
La Barge £–££
Floating on the Rhône, look out over the river while eating tapas – perhaps 'the indecision' tasting selection – and drinking cocktails.
Quai Sarrail.
La Ferme de Monplaisir £–££
In summer, this restaurant sprawls into the courtyard, while winter sees a more intimate setting in the homely dining room. The food is rustic and farm-themed.
64 rue des Frères Lumières.
Tel: (04) 78 75 00 00.

ENTERTAINMENT
Hangar du Premier Film
This is the factory building outside which the Lumières filmed the world's first film – of workers leaving in 1895. Visitors can enter through that very doorway, looking up at the beams of the original factory, into the cinema that has been built in and around the vestiges of the old building.
23 rue du Premier Film.
Tel: 0892 68 88 79.
www.institut-lumiere.org.
Open: Tue–Sun.

SPORT AND LEISURE
Piscine d'été du Rhône
These two alfresco Olympic-sized pools, one for laps and the other for larking, are a popular place to sunbathe or cool down, with lifeguards and child-friendly areas.
8 quai Claude Bernard.
Tel: (04) 78 72 04 50.
Open: Jun–beginning of Sept. Admission charge.

Beaujolais
ACCOMMODATION
Les Roulottes de la Serve £–££
A different camping experience, with restored and refurbished gypsy caravans set in a field among trees. Breakfast included.
La Serve, 69680 Auroux.
Tel: (04) 74 04 76 40.
www.lesroulottes.com.
Open: Apr–Oct.

L'Auberge du Paradis £££
A beautiful hotel with seven individualistic rooms, Jacuzzi, small swimming pool and high-quality restaurant offering an interesting monthly set menu.
Le Plâtre Durand, Saint-Amour.
Tel: (03) 85 37 10 26.
www.aubergeduparadis.fr.
Restaurant open: Wed–Sun.
Château de Bagnols ££££
Five-star deluxe hotel in a fully restored 13th-century château complete with Renaissance wall and ceiling paintings, dry moat and drawbridge, plus a Michelin-starred restaurant.
69620 Bagnols.
Tel: (04) 74 71 40 00.
www.chateaudebagnols.fr

EATING OUT
L'Auberge Vigneronne ££
A picturesque eatery with pleasant outdoor seating, serving traditional and regional specialities made from local produce.
Le Bourg, 69430 Régnié-Durette. Tel: (04) 74 04

35 95. Closed: Mon & Tue evenings & 20 Dec–20 Jan.

Le Donjon ££

In the golden-stone village of Oingt, Le Donjon enjoys a panoramic prospect over the Beaujolais countryside. Frogs are a speciality.

64 petite rue du Marché, Oingt.
Tel: (04) 74 71 20 24.
Open: Thur–Mon.

SPORT AND LEISURE

Excelys Tours

This Lyon-based company offers personalised, informative tours by friendly and knowledgeable guides within the region and across France.

Tel: (04) 72 59 28 13.
www.excelystours.fr

Velo Rail du Bugey

This company rents out 'Cyclos' to ride on the disused railway lines. Two people pedal and two or three sit in between.

46 avenue de la Gare, Pugieu Bugey.
Tel: (04) 79 87 84 94.
www.velorail01.
pagesperso-orange.fr

East and south of Lyon

ACCOMMODATION

Grand Hôtel De La Poste ££

A well-kept hotel in an old coach house situated in the centre of Vienne. Free Wi-Fi and parking.

47 cours Romestang, Vienne.
Tel: (04) 74 85 02 04.

NH Lyon Aeroport ££–£££

This thoroughly modern 4-star airport hotel with 24-hour reception offers travellers a comfortable place to bed down for the night and beat the traffic to mountain resorts next morning.

Terminal 1, Lyon-Saint Exupéry. Tel: (04) 72 23 05 50. www.nh-hotels.com

EATING OUT

L'Hostellerie £££–££££

In the heart of the walled town of Pérouges, local specialities such as crayfish and Bresse chicken are served by waiters in period costume in this medieval inn.

Place du Tilleul, Pérouges.
Tel: (04) 74 61 00 88.
hostelleriedeperouges.com

SPORT AND LEISURE

Sorties Nature et Patrimoine

The tourist office arranges two-hour guided themed walks of the Dombes for a minimal charge (free for under-12s).

Office de Tourisme, Villard-les-Dombes.
Tel: (04) 74 98 06 29.
Open: May–Sept.

GRENOBLE AND ISÈRE

Grenoble and around

ACCOMMODATION

Hôtel de l'Europe ££

Grenoble's oldest hotel has been given a modern facelift and is very reasonable for its fantastic location. The star rating is based on fully en-suite rooms, but there are cheaper alternatives with shared bathrooms. All have free Wi-Fi.

22 place Grenette.
Tel: (04) 76 46 16 94.
www.hoteleurope.fr

Mercure Grenoble Grand Hôtel Président ££

Staying in a chain hotel can be a good choice in Grenoble and this one

has a pool, copious breakfast buffet and good location for excursions.
11 rue Général Mangin. Tel: (04) 76 56 26 56. www.accorhotels.com

Splendid Hotel ££
Located in a quiet side street close to the city centre, this unpretentious hotel is pleasant and bright. Car park, garden, and Wi-Fi in the bedrooms are all bonuses.
22 rue Thiers. Tel: (04) 76 46 33 12. www.splendid-hotel.com

EATING OUT

Au Bureau £–££
The large *salades à composer* (pick-and-choose your ingredients) are an inspired feature of the menu at this casual café-bar.
8–10 place Grenette. Tel: (04) 76 44 00 40.

Le Tonneau de Diogène £–££
With a cellar-like dining area at the back, a classic bar at the front and a philosophical bookshop downstairs, Le Tonneau de Diogène is an atmospheric café. Pavement seating, Wi-Fi, chess sets and

continuous service, including on Sundays, add to its laid-back appeal.
6 place Notre-Dame. Tel: (04) 76 42 38 40.

Café de la Table Ronde ££
Open for business since 1739, this venerable institution has an extensive menu of classic regional and national dishes.
7 place Saint-André. Tel: (04) 76 44 51 41. www.restaurant-tableronde-grenoble.com (in French). Open: Mon–Sat 7am–midnight.

La Fondue ££
Celebrates the famous dish in an array of varieties, plus other mountain staples. The wood-clad décor, featuring old-fashioned skis, reflects the theme.
5 rue Brocherie. Tel: (04) 76 15 20 72. Open: Tue–Sat lunch & dinner, Mon dinner only.

ENTERTAINMENT

La Boîte à Sardines
Although small, the 'Sardine Tin' is actually a bright and breezy bar, with large windows and a

terrace to spill on to. The *cocktail du jour* is a bargain choice.
1 place Claveyson. Tel: (04) 76 44 27 84.

Le Club
Cinema showing international films in original-language versions.
9 rue du Phalanstère. Tel: (04) 76 87 46 21.

MC2
Grenoble's leading entertainment centre, MC2 puts on a varied programme of theatre, music and dance events.
Maison de la Culture, 4 rue Paul Claudel. Tel: (04) 76 00 79 00. www.mc2.grenoble.fr. Box office open: Tue–Fri 12.30–7pm, Sat 2–7pm.

La Soupe au Choux
Open since 1982, this jazz club has built up quite a reputation and showcases a range of styles. Live music at 9pm, and dinner served before the show.
7 route de Lyon. Tel: (04) 76 87 05 67. www.jazzalasoupe.free.fr. Open: Tue–Sat 8pm–1am. Admission charge.

SPORT AND LEISURE

Bureau des Guides et Accompagnateurs de Grenoble

Join a group excursion or book a guide independently for any sort of mountain activity. *Maison de la Montagne. Tel: (04) 38 37 01 71. www.guide-grenoble.com (in French).*

Club Nautique de Cholonge

Affiliated to the École Française de Voile (French Sailing School), this Lac Laffrey club offers lessons and weekly courses on weekdays. *Tel: (04) 76 83 08 35.*

Le Vercors

ACCOMMODATION

Le Millepertuis £

Filled to capacity, this eight-person self-catering chalet is a bargain. It has a wood-burning stove and large deck, and is convenient for the village centre and skiing. Minimum stay two nights. *Corrençon-en-Vercors. Tel: (04) 76 40 79 40.*

Le Gerbier £–££

Summer guests can take advantage of a nice garden and village-centre location. Winter guests have free shuttles to the ski runs. Full- and half-board options. *158 avenue Général de Gaulle, Villard-de-Lans. Tel: (04) 76 95 10 50. www.hotel-le-gerbier.com*

EATING OUT

Le Bois Fleuri £££–££££

Recently Michelin-starred, this is more than a hotel restaurant, with chef Jérome Faure presiding. There is also an impressive wine list full of rare and unusual vintages. *Les Ritons, Corrençon-en-Vercors. Tel: (04) 76 95 84 84. www.hotel-du-golf-vercors.fr*

SPORT AND LEISURE

Colline des Bains

Good for kids or just for fun, there is a choice of sledge, from toboggan to rubber ring, and different tracks to slide down, including a dug tube that acts as a miniature bobsleigh course. *Avenue des Bains, Villard-de-Lans. Tel: (04) 76 56 97 29.*

Massif de la Chartreuse

ACCOMMODATION

La Ferme Bonne de la Grotte

This '*gite panda*' (conservation-focused accommodation) on the Savoie edge of the park consists of a grouping of barn conversions, with heart-themed interiors. *Saint-Christophe-la-Grotte. Tel: (04) 79 36 59 05. www.gites-savoie.com/sejour/eco-gite*

EATING OUT

La Ferme Brévardière ££

At the foot of the monastery, this farmhouse restaurant serves foods from their own and neighbouring smallholdings. Reservations are necessary. You can also request a summer picnic basket with bread, cheese and salad. *Saint-Hugues, Saint-Pierre-de-Chartreuse. Tel: (04) 76 88 60 49. www.brevardiere.fr. Open: daily for dinner, Thur–Tue for lunch.*

SPORT AND LEISURE

Cartusiana

Cartusiana organises walks for individuals and

groups along the many trails laced across the Chartreuse.

Place de la Mairie, Saint-Pierre-de-Chartreuse. Tel: (04) 38 86 91 31. www.cartusiana.com

Spéléo-Canyon Chartreuse

Discover the hidden caves of Chartreuse and explore canyons and waterfalls with guide Julien Cero. Full- or half-days are available for all skill levels.

Les Thévenons, Saint-Franc. Tel: 06 60 86 68 39. www.speleo-canyon-chartreuse.fr

L'Alpe d'Huez and Les Deux Alpes

ACCOMMODATION

Les 2 Alpes Réservation

This accommodation service is available on the phone and online (with an English version) and covers the full range of accommodation.

Office de Tourisme, Les 2 Alpes. Tel: (04) 76 79 24 38. www.les2alpes.com. Open: Mon–Sat 9am–noon & 2–6pm.

La Perle de L'Oisans Apartments ££

Ten luxury self-catering apartments managed by

UK company Ski Peak. They are typically booked as part of a package, but the star rating is based on the accommodation-only option.

Vaujany, Alpe d'Huez. Tel: +44 (0)1428 608 070. www.skipeak.net

EATING OUT

Chalet du Lac Besson ££

In winter, on the edge of a frozen lake just off a cross-country ski route, warmth is to be had through the medium of stew, hot cheese and a blazing fire.

Piste Boulevard des Lacs, Alpe d'Huez. Tel: (04) 76 80 65 37.

Smithy's Tavern ££

Tex-Mex in massive portions, with vegetarian options and children's menus. Reserve ahead. The lively bar has draught beers including Guinness.

Route du Coulet, Alpe d'Huez. Tel: (04) 76 11 32 29. www.smithystavern.com. Open: Mon–Fri from 5pm, Sat from 10am, Sun from 2.30pm.

Tribeca Caffé ££

An Italian restaurant serving pizzas cooked

in a traditional stone oven. Matching the second-hand furniture is an equally vintage wine list.

9 route de Champamé, Les Deux Alpes. Tel: (04) 76 80 58 53. www.letribeca.com

Le Charbon de Bois £££

The name refers to cooking done over charcoal and they cook up an array of regional specialities. Enjoy the terrace in summer and the fireplace in winter.

8 rue du Grand Plan, Les Deux Alpes. Tel: (04) 76 80 57 42. www.restaurant-lecharbondebois.com

ENTERTAINMENT

Smokey Joe's

This hotspot at the base of the main ski lift shows sport on the big screen, has a comprehensive drinks menu, and stays open into the small hours.

Le Meijotel, Les Deux Alpes. Tel: (04) 76 79 28 97. www.smokey.joes. pagesperso-orange.fr

The Underground

Underneath the Hôtel le Chamois, skiers converge

at this fun and popular bar with live music.
Chemin de la Chapelle, L'Alpe-d'Huez. Tel: (04) 76 80 31 19.

SPORT AND LEISURE
Bureau des Guides et Accompagnateurs des 2 Alpes
The team of guides runs rock- and ice-climbing courses and leads excursions on foot, skis and snowshoes.
Place des Deux Alpes. Tel: (04) 76 11 36 29. www.guides2alpes.com
Eclose Ice Driving Circuit
This is 856m (2,808ft) of track used by professional race-car drivers. Lessons are given for beginners and the more experienced in the art of ice racing.
Rue du 93ème R A M, Alpe d'Huez. Tel: 06 08 06 67 22. www.evodriver.fr

Chaîne de Belledonne
ACCOMMODATION
Auberge de Jeunesse Le Recoin £
A great budget choice, dorm rates at this hostel include breakfast;

various activities can be arranged and there is even a small sauna and Jacuzzi.
20 rue des Alisiers, Chamrousse. Tel: (04) 76 89 91 31 / (04) 76 89 96 66. www.fuaj.org/Chamrousse
Les Granges de Sept Laux ££
Rent apartments for two to twelve within a traditional-style chalet at the foot of the slopes, with spa area and restaurant. The residence can arrange ski hire and lift passes.
Prapoutel. Tel: (04) 76 78 31 55. www.les7laux immobilierservices.com

EATING OUT
L'Écureuil ££
Having been in Chamrousse since before it became a ski station, this family restaurant is well established. Their classic menus combine local favourites with house specialities.
128 place de Belledonne, Le Recoin, Chamrousse. Tel: (04) 76 89 90 13. www. lecureuilchamrousse.com

SPORT AND LEISURE
Chlorophile
Small company of mountain guides who can arrange tree climbing at equipped sites, plus walking with donkeys in summer and snowshoes in winter.
Prapoutel, Sept Laux. Tel: 06 63 38 34 74. www.chlorophile.org (in French).

SAVOIE
Les Trois Vallées
ACCOMMODATION
Les Fermes de Méribel ££
Residence of 90 contemporary apartments of 2 to 5 rooms (4–10 or 11 people), with kitchens and balconies. Swimming pool, spa, disabled access, Wi-Fi and reception.
Méribel-Village. Tel: (04) 79 01 32 00. www.pierreetvacances.com
Hôtel L'Olympic ££–£££
A more affordable option in the centre of luxurious Couchevel 1850, this hotel is simple but has the necessary essentials and breakfast included.
Rue des Tovets, Courchevel 1850.

Tel: (04) 79 65 07 65.

Résidence L'Oxalys £££

Worlds away from standard self-catering ski accommodation, these upmarket chalet-style apartments for two to eight people are spacious, trendily designed and have on-site luxury features (pools, saunas, Michelin-starred restaurant).

Entrée station, Val Thorens.
Tel: (04) 79 10 49 15.
www.montagnettes.com

EATING OUT
La Ferme de Reberty ££

A popular restaurant and bar where good quality is matched by good value and a friendly atmosphere.

Reberty, Les Menuires.
Tel: (04) 79 00 77 01.

La Table de Mon Grand-Père ££–£££

The restaurant of the classic mountain hotel Les Peupliers, serving up traditional dishes with gourmet contemporary twists. A fireplace in winter and a terrace in summer create seasonal mountain ambience.

Hôtel les Peupliers,

Courchevel 1300/La Praz.
Tel: (04) 79 08 41 42.

ENTERTAINMENT
Le Chabichou

Serves pastry and cakes in the morning, morphs into a tapas bar at 5pm. Jazz on Wednesdays.

Courchevel. Tel: (04) 79 08 00 55. www.chabichou-courchevel.com

Malaysia

Lively late-night basement nightclub with DJs and live bands.

15 place Caron, Val Thorens. Tel: (04) 79 00 05 25.
www.lemalaysia.com

Rond Point

Super-popular bar-restaurant at the bottom of the lifts, with live music on the large terrace from 5–7pm.

Méribel. Tel: (04) 79 00 37 51. www. rondpointmeribel.com

SPORT AND LEISURE
Bureau des Guides de Courchevel

The guides run canyoning courses from €42, climbing lessons and courses progressing from artificial walls to real mountains, plus

various other activities.

Tel: 06 23 92 46 12.
www.guides-courchevel.fr

Val Thorens Toboggan

Tickets for this exhilarating 6km (3¾-mile) course cost €12 (€18 without a lift pass) and include mulled wine and local cheese. Children aged 5–10 ride for free.

Toboggan Chalet, Maison de Val Thorens. Tel: (04) 79 00 08 08. Open: 10am–3pm, plus evenings Wed–Fri.

Espace Killy
ACCOMMODATION
Chalet Colinn £££

Rooms can be rented individually (half board) or groups of 10–14 can take the whole chalet. A weekly accommodation plus lift-pass package is available along with shuttle service to the ski resort. Sauna and Norwegian bath are included.

Le Franchet, Tignes.
Tel: (04) 79 06 26 99.
www.chaletcolinn.com

Hôtel Ormelune £££–££££

Every bit of this friendly hotel, from the spacious

rooms (modern furnishings with splashes of vivid colour) to the corridors (grass-patterned carpets and a large cow sculpture on every floor), is an ode to originality. The artistic lounge-bar invites non-guests too to enjoy a drink by the modern fireplace.
Val d'Isère. Tel: (04) 79 06 12 93. www.ormelune.com

Le Tsanteleina £££–££££
Classy, traditional and with a welcoming staff team, it is easy to see why guests return to this hotel, run by the same family for several generations. It was recently extended to include a fabulous spa. Free Wi-Fi available.
Val d'Isère.
Tel: (04) 79 06 12 13. www.tsanteleina.com

Eating out
Le Salon des Fous £
A cute tearoom serving breakfast, lunch, crêpes and drinks.
Val d'Isère. Tel: (04) 79 00 17 92. Open: daily 8am–9.30pm.

Lo Soli ££
Offers a delicious mix of Italian and French fare

along with an epic view over Espace Killy and the Grande Motte glacier.
Top of Chaudannes chairlift, Tignes.
Tel: (04) 79 06 98 63.
Open: winter.

La Table des Neiges £££
The elegant restaurant of the Tsanteleina hotel does meals to savour, from the dainty *amuse-bouches* through the delicious gourmet regional starters and mains to the local cheeses and mouthwatering desserts.
Val d'Isère, see 'Le Tsanteleina' above.

Entertainment
Alpaka cocktail bar
Over 100 cocktail options, international spirits, draught beers, happy hour all night Sunday and live music by local bands make this an excellent après-ski venue.
4 monteé du Rosset, Tignes. Tel: (04) 79 06 45 30. www.alpaka.com

Warm up
A comfortable English-language bar, with pool table, snacks, cocktails and free Wi-Fi. Gets

lively from when the lifts close into the night.
Val d'Isère. Tel: (04) 79 08 27 00. www. warmupvaldisere.com. Open: winter season.

Sport and leisure
Oxygen Centre Aquasportif
Swimming pool, sauna, steam bath, Jacuzzi, squash courts and fitness classes on offer; different rates apply.
Val d'Isère. Tel: (04) 79 04 26 01. www.oxygen-valdisere.com

Paradiski and Bourg-Saint-Maurice
Accommodation
Hôtel Angival ££
With comfortable rooms, including several family rooms, this traditional hotel is good for a quiet stay near the funicular to Les Arcs.
90 rue Jean Moulin, Bourg-Saint-Maurice.
Tel: (04) 79 07 27 97.

Chalet Béguin ££–£££
A pleasant ski-in ski-out location, with both hotel rooms and apartments. Room-only is available in summer; winter stays are half board.

Village des Deux Têtes,
Arc 1600.
Tel: (04) 79 07 02 92.
www.chalet-beguin.com

Hôtel et Spa La
Tourmaline ££–£££
Acts as a comfortable
and attractive base
camp from which to
explore the surrounding
slopes, with deals on
ski and bobsleigh
passes.
175 route de la Fortune,
Aime la Plagne. Tel: (04)
79 55 62 93. www.hotel-
tourmaline.com

EATING OUT
La Bohème ££
The French and
international menu is
interestingly varied, and
for afternoon tea there is
an assortment of world
teas, coffee and cakes.
Villards, Arc 1800. Tel:
(04) 79 41 99 43. www.
laboheme-lesarcs.com

Le Refuge Alt. 810 ££
Fondue and raclette are
popular choices, but
there are also more
unusual options, plus
vegetarian and children's
menus.
55 Grande-Rue, Bourg-
Saint-Maurice.
Tel: (04) 79 07 52 54.

ENTERTAINMENT
Le J O Live Rock Café
With live music and a
friendly upbeat vibe, the
J O is open late into the
small hours.
Galerie de la Poste (le
Charvet), Arc 1800.
Tel: (04) 79 07 40 42.

La Mine
The best spot in Plagne
1800, this place has live
music in themed décor.
La Plagne 1800.
Tel: (04) 79 09 24 89.

SPORT AND LEISURE
Association Bob/Luge
Following in the glide-
tracks of the 1992
Olympic bobsleighs on
La Plagne's famous run
costs €38, but special
offers are available.
Piste Olympique de
Bobsleigh, La Roche,
Mâcot-la-Plagne.
Tel: (04) 79 09 12 73.
www.bobsleigh.net

Valmorel
ACCOMMODATION
Hôtel du Bourg ££–£££
This standard mountain
hotel is good value in
summer, pricey in winter,
but boasts a spa and
great location by the
ski lifts.

Rue Bourg-Morel,
Valmorel.
Tel: (04) 79 09 86 66.
www.hoteldubourg.com

EATING OUT
Le Petit Prince ££
Perfectly representing the
archetypal image of a
mountain restaurant, this
inviting place does both
standard and less well-
known regional
specialities, plus a
children's menu.
7 rue Bourg-Morel.
Tel: (04) 79 09 81 71.
www.restaurant-
lepetitprince.com

SPORT AND LEISURE
La Diligence
Horse and pony activities
including treks and
sleigh rides through
the snow.
L'Aigle Blanc, Valmorel.
Tel: (04) 79 09 90 07.
Open: 9.30am–12.30pm
& 1.30–5pm.

Aix-les-Bains and Lac
du Bourget
ACCOMMODATION
Hôtel Palais des
Fleurs ££
A short walk from the
centre of Aix, this is a
pleasant hotel with

swimming pool, sauna and Wi-Fi access. Various accommodation and leisure packages are available.

17 rue Isaline, Aix-les-Bains.
Tel: (04) 79 88 35 08.

EATING OUT

La Grange à Sel £££

Stone walls, wooden beams, soft lighting and an open fire set a romantic mood at this 17th-century salt barn turned restaurant. The creative market menu of the day is a bargain.

La Croix Verte, Le Bourget-du-Lac.
Tel: (04) 79 25 02 66.
www.lagrangeasel.com.
Open: Feb–Dec. Closed: Wed & Sun dinner.

ENTERTAINMENT

Casino Grand Cercle

Dating from 1847, this impressive building contains not only the requisite blackjack tables, but also bars, a restaurant, a nightclub and an opulent 850-seat theatre.

20 rue du Casino, Aix-les-Bains. Tel: (04) 79 35 16 16. www. casinograndcercle.com

Maurienne

ACCOMMODATION

Chalet des Eterlous ££

Self-catering apartments of varying sizes rest in a calm setting an easy walk from conveniences such as the tourist office, ski school and chairlift.

Vieux Village, Bonneval-sur-Arc. Tel: (04) 79 05 94 52. www.les-eterlous.com

EATING OUT

Le Pontet £–££

Typical Savoyard fare including fondue, raclette and tartiflette, served up in the authentic setting of Bonneval village.

Bonneval-sur-Arc.
Tel: (04) 79 05 95 50.

La Grange de Thelcide ££

Reliable casual meals, such as savoury and sweet crêpes, omelettes and salads, are the order of the day at this rustic café-restaurant.

Rue des Grandes Alpes, Valloire.
Tel: (04) 79 59 06 62.

SPORT AND LEISURE

Snowpark Valloire Galibier

Boarders in particular will enjoy the free-style fun at this playground of curves, jumps and rails with a World Cup-sized half-pipe. A snowpark pass is €16 per day.

Lac de la Vieille, Valloire.
Open: 10am–5pm.

Chambéry and Massif des Bauges

ACCOMMODATION

L'École de Glaise £

A *gîte panda* located in the Massif des Bauges offering the option of room-only, B&B and half or full board, all bargains.

2623 route de Saint-Ruph, Faverges.
Tel: (04) 56 16 43 41.
www.giteglaise. chez-alice.fr (in French).

La Ferme du Petit Bonheur ££

Beautiful in all seasons, this 18th-century farmhouse is ten minutes' walk from Chambéry and ideally situated for exploring the neighbouring wilds.

538 chemin de Jean-Jacques, Chambéry.
Tel: (04) 79 85 26 17.
www. fermedupetitbonheur.fr

EATING OUT

Brasserie Le Z £

Intriguing set menus full of fresh and fruity cuisine change daily, complemented by a quality wine list. The adjacent bar serves cocktails plus some rare cognacs in comfort from 6pm.

12 avenue des Ducs de Savoie, Chambéry. Tel: (04) 79 85 96 87. www.zorelle.fr (in French).

Le Bar à Thym £–££

This bright and breezy organic restaurant does healthy vegetable-rich meals and assorted fresh juices.

22 place Monge, Chambéry. Tel: (04) 79 70 96 40. Open: Tue–Sat (Tue & Wed daytime only). barathym.fr

SPORT AND LEISURE

Vertes Sensations

Canoe or kayak on the serene lake, with advice on different routes to paddle and rentals from €7.

North Lac d'Aiguebelette. Tel: (04) 79 28 77 08. Open: Apr–Oct; rest of the year with a reservation.

HAUTE-SAVOIE

Chamonix and Mont Blanc area

ACCOMMODATION

Camping les Deux Glaciers £

Large campsite with 150 pitches, some heated mini-chalets, free Wi-Fi, heated shower areas, laundry and restaurant. Guests are given a free public transport pass (central Chamonix is a bus ride away).

80 route des Tissières. Tel: (04) 50 53 15 84. www.les2glaciers.com. Open: mid-Dec–mid-Nov.

Hôtel and Chalet du Bois ££

Apartments for two to ten people, as well as interconnecting hotel rooms, make this an ideal choice for families seeking a quiet Chamonix valley location. Bonuses include a garden with a fantastic view of the Mont Blanc massif, spa, and indoor and outdoor pools. Buffet breakfasts and dinners are extra.

475 avenue des Alpages, 74310 Les Houches. Tel: (04) 50 54 50 35. www.hotel-du-bois.com

Hameau Albert 1er ££££

This cool, classy hotel 'hamlet' encompasses a main building, 15 outhouses and a chalet arranged around a garden, all tastefully designed. The spa, bar and restaurants, Albert 1er (with two Michelin stars) and La Maison Carrier (seasonal classic cuisine), are top quality.

38 route du Bouchet, Chamonix. Tel: (04) 50 53 05 09. www.hameaualbert.fr

EATING OUT

Berlucoquet £

Proving that good things can come in small packages, this wine cellar-bar-sandwich shop is packed to the rafters with bottles and goodies. Their interesting sandwich fillings make a change from the standard ham and cheese.

98 avenue de l'Aiguille du Midi, Chamonix.

Café de l'Arve ££

Local seasonal produce (including Lac Léman fish, meat from nearby farms and market fruit and vegetables) is styled into imaginative dishes at this funky and fresh café-restaurant.

60 impasse des Anémones. Tel: (04) 50 53 58 57. www.cafe-arve.com

L'Impossible ££–£££

Since the Italian Bucci family relocated from Courmayeur to Chamonix, a loyal band of customers has been crossing the border to keep dining with them, a testament to the originality of the healthy, organic cuisine produced by Auro Bucci and Japanese co-chef Takeshi Minagawa. Meat-eaters, vegetarians and vegans are all catered for in a romantic old farmhouse building.

Route des Pèlerins, Chamonix. Tel: (04) 50 53 20 36. www.restaurant-impossible.com. Open: Tue–Fri 6.30–10pm, Sat–Sun noon–3pm & 6.30–10pm.

ENTERTAINMENT

Bar La Calèche

Pavement seating on one of Megève's prettiest squares, with an outdoor mulled-wine bar to warm up in winter, plus aperitifs and tapas in the indoor lounge. Casual meals, ice cream and smoothies are also served.

Place de l'Église, 4 rue Monseigneur Conseil, Mégève. Tel: (04) 50 58 99 13. www.barlacaleche.fr

Chambre Neuf

Lively bar opposite the main railway station in Chamonix.

272 avenue Michel Croz. Tel: (04) 50 55 89 81. Open: 8am–1am.

Cinéma Vox

Screens English-language films in the original version.

Cour Bartavel, Chamonix. Tel: (04) 50 53 03 39. www.chamonix.com

SPORT AND LEISURE

Les Ailes du Mont Blanc

Professional paragliding school offering tandem flights around Mont Blanc, plus 'discovery' days and longer courses.

24 avenue de la Plage, Chamonix. Tel: (04) 50 53 96 72. www. lesailesdumontblanc.com

Annecy and Lac d'Annecy

ACCOMMODATION

L'Auberge du Lyonnais £–££

Delightful in style and location, right on the canal front in old Annecy, this little hotel is a bargain.

9 rue de la République, Annecy. Tel: (04) 50 51 26 10. www.auberge-du-lyonnais.com

Les Trésoms £££

A beautiful lake view and secluded setting make it well worth the uphill climb from central Annecy, with a luxurious spa, outdoor pool, sun terrace and leafy garden adding to the charms. The hotel has eco-credentials too: most of the water is heated by solar collectors.

3 boulevard de la Corniche. Tel: (04) 50 51 43 84. www.lestresoms.com

EATING OUT

Edelweiss £–££

At the top of the Col de la Forclaz, this hotel café-restaurant serves up meals, snacks, drinks and ice creams, accompanied by a spectacular view over the lake.

Col de la Forclaz, Montmin.
Tel: (04) 50 60 70 24.
www.sav.org/edelweiss

L'Étage ££

Authentic traditional restaurant located on one of the quieter streets of the Old Town. Among the regional specialities on the menu is *farçon*, a fried potato cake with bacon and dates, as well as the better-known classics of fondue, raclette and tartiflette.
3 rue du Pacquier. Tel: (04) 50 51 03 28.

Les Trésoms La Rotonde £££–££££

The gourmet restaurant of Les Trésoms is a truly memorable place to dine. Chef Benjamin Collombat combines artistic presentation with a wonderfully inventive blend of flavours, and a stunning view over the lake completes the experience.
See 'Les Trésoms' above.

ENTERTAINMENT

Café des Ducs

The main attraction of this bar is the close-up view of the Palais de l'Île. They serve ice creams and snacks alongside drinks.
Quai des Vieilles Prisons.
Tel: (04) 50 65 08 14.

Finn Kelly's

Tucked away in a backstreet, this Irish-style pub stays open late daily and is a good place for a quiet pint.
10 faubourg des Annonciades.
Tel: (04) 50 51 29 40.

Théâtre d'Annecy

Spectacles of all sorts are staged at Annecy's dynamic theatre.
Centre Bonlieu, 1 rue Jean-Jaurès.
Tel: (04) 50 33 44 11.
www.bonlieu-annecy.com

SPORT AND LEISURE

Delta Evasion

Soar over Lac d'Annecy, either paragliding or hang-gliding from the Col de la Forclaz or in an ultra-light from Doussard, south of the lake.
Col de la Forclaz.
Tel: (04) 50 60 25 85.
Doussard tel: 06 08 32 49 59.
www.deltaevasion.com

Société des Régates à Voile d'Annecy

Sailing school offering a range of lessons and courses.
31 rue des Marquisats.
Tel: (04) 50 45 48 39.
www.srva.info. Open: Mar–Oct Mon–Sat 9am–noon & 1–5pm.

Lac Léman

ACCOMMODATION

Au Pré des Ânes £–££

A small eco-*gîte* in a renovated farm which retains its donkeys. It includes rooms adapted for people with reduced mobility or who are partially sighted. Dinner features food from the garden and fish from the lake cooked in local style.
Chez Portay, Feternes. Tel: (04) 50 81 03 45 / 06 14 17 70 76. www.leman-chambres-hotes.com (in French).

Hilton Évian ££–£££

One of the large grand hotels facing the lake, the Hilton is continuously open and has a great swimming pool and spacious rooms.
Quai Paul Leger, Évian-les-Bains.

Tel: (04) 50 84 60 00.
www.hilton.co.uk/evian

La Verniaz et ses Chalets £££

Once a 17th-century farm, La Verniaz is now a hotel and collection of chalets, arranged around a lovely flower-filled garden. Just a short drive from Évian, it has a peaceful country setting in between the lake and the Chablais hills. The gastronomic restaurant beckons with seasonal market menus or a spit roast from the garden. Local wines and international whiskies are on the bar list.
Route d'Abondance, Neuvecelle-Église, 74500 Évian-les-Bains.
Tel: (04) 50 75 04 90.
www.verniaz.com.
Open: Feb–early Nov.

EATING OUT
Le Muratore £–££

The options at this central Évian restaurant include gourmet salads, seafood and lake fish dishes. The teatime menu is a plus for hungry sightseers.
Place Jean Bernex, Évian-les-Bains. Tel: (04) 50 92

82 49. Open: Tue & Sun 11.45am–5pm, Wed–Sat 11.45am–5pm & 7–9.30pm.

Restaurant La Perche ££

As suggested by the name, this restaurant specialises in perch from the lake, although traditional Savoyard favourites are offered too. The terrace is shaded by a tree canopy.
Rue de l'Église, Yvoire. Tel: (04) 50 72 89 30. Open Feb–mid-Oct.

ENTERTAINMENT
Café le Brummel's

One of several pavement bar-cafés on bustling Rue Nationale, this inviting bar has Wi-Fi access and serves coffee, tea and snacks as well as drinks such as house punch.
30 rue Nationale, Évian-les-Bains.
Tel: (04) 50 75 37 13.

Portes du Soleil
ACCOMMODATION
Chalet Philibert £££–££££

The wooden-beamed rooms are cute, snug and classically Alpine. An outdoor pool and fitness area are bonuses in the

summer. A 20-minute walk from the town centre, accommodation is on a half-board basis in winter, with room-only in summer.
480 route des Putheys, Morzine. Tel: (04) 50 79 25 18. www.chalet-philibert.com

Hôtel le Samoyède £££–££££

Chalet-style hotel in the heart of Morzine. Each room is individual and there is a range of sizes, with family rooms like mini-chalets. Check for special offers.
9 place du Baraty, Morzine. Tel: (04) 50 79 00 79. www.hotel-lesamoyede.com

SYM Concept

Determined to make mountain holidays accessible to all, SYM Concept arranges all-inclusive holidays in Morzine and Avoriaz for travellers with physical disabilities. As well as booking accommodation, they organise activities.
592 route de la Combe à Zore, Morzine.
Tel: 0811 03 75 09.
www.symconcept.com

EATING OUT
L'Atelier £££

In the talented hands of chef Alexandre Baud-Pachon, son of the hotel owners, Le Samoyède's restaurant has become a top Morzine dining address. The menu changes monthly, but tasty and imaginatively conceived dishes are guaranteed.

9 place du Baraty. Tel: (04) 50 79 00 79.

La Chamade £££

In the welcoming space of this family-run restaurant, chef Thierry Thorens' take on mountain cuisine involves making creative use of local produce. Pork is a speciality, but vegetables, fruits and herbs take centre stage too. The inventive use of ingredients extends to the presentation: each dish is a colourful feast for the eyes as well as the stomach (and portions are huge).

90 route de la Plagne, Morzine. Tel: (04) 50 79 13 91. www.lachamade.com

ENTERTAINMENT
Le Chapka

Pool tables, live music and huge TV screens contribute to the popularity of this bar, open until 2am at busy times. Light meals and snacks are available too.

Village de la Falaise, 35 rue du Douchka, Avoriaz. Tel: (04) 50 74 23 30.

Le Coup du Coeur

Opposite La Chamade restaurant and under the same management, this new bar is a great addition to Morzine nightlife. The indoor lounge bar is both cosy and trendy, while the garden area is perfect for summer evenings.

Route de la Plagne, Morzine. Open: 8.30am–1am.

SPORT AND LEISURE
École MCF Synergie

Adults and children of all levels of proficiency can join this mountain-bike school for lessons, courses and guided tours of Morzine/Les Gets.

Twinner Morzna, Rond Point de la Clusaz, Morzine. Tel: 06 87 39 00 14. www.synergie-vtt.com

Massif des Aravis
ACCOMMODATION
Les Ecotagnes ££££

Sleep in one of two tree-house cabins with deck space and wood-burning stoves, containing several double rooms and an environmentally friendly hot tub. Rates include breakfast and dinner, plus in winter also afternoon tea, after-dinner activities (snowscooter/snow walk) and coffee in the teepee.

Between Les Villards-sur-Thônes & La Clusaz. Tel: 06 70 02 10 14. www.ecotagnes.com

EATING OUT
La Scierie ££

This welcoming restaurant is housed in an old sawmill building ('La Scierie' means 'The Sawmill'). The seasonal cuisine combines tradition with originality and includes gourmet platters, nourishing mountain meals and children's menus.

321–331 route du Col des Aravis, La Clusaz. Tel: (04) 50 63 34 68.

*www.la-scierie.com.
Open: summer 11am–
3pm & 6pm–midnight;
winter 11am–midnight.*

Compagnie des Guides Aravis

With centres in La Clusaz and Le Grand Bornand, the guides lead activities including climbing and mountain biking in summer; snowshoe walks and cross-country skiing in winter.
Tel: (04) 50 63 35 99 (La Clusaz) / (04) 50 02 78 18 (Le Grand Bornand). www.compagnie-des-guides-aravis.com

Faucigny
ACCOMMODATION
Chalets Hameau de Flaine £–££

In a quiet self-contained hamlet above Flaine, these self-catering chalets enjoy a picturesque view. Most rent by the week, and prices vary as they are individually owned.
Galerie Marchande, Flaine Forum. Tel: (04) 50 90 46 70. www. flaineimmobilier.com

Hotel Restaurant Les Glaciers ££–£££

A three-star hotel, a mere eight minutes from skiing in the Grand Massif, with a heated swimming pool open to the sky in good weather and covered in bad, plus a lounge bar.
Le Bourg, Samoëns. Tel: (04) 50 34 40 06. www.hotel-les-glaciers.com

EATING OUT
Restaurant La Tornalta ££

Typical Savoyard fare, with all things cheese-based though there is also a selection of meat dishes, in an old building on the corner of the square.
Rue Parc, Samoëns. Tel: (04) 50 34 98 68.

ENTERTAINMENT
Le Bois de Lune

Vibrant cocktail bar with comfy lounge seating and a restaurant on site too.
Le Quart, Samoëns. Tel: (04) 50 34 18 02.

SPORT AND LEISURE
Évasion Nordique

Learn to drive your own little pack of dogs, for an hour or half day (€55/ €10).
Les Carroz, Flaine. Tel: 06 82 09 50 03. www. evasion-nordique.com

SOUTHERN ALPS
Briançonnais
ACCOMMODATION
Hôtel Ibis ££

Reasonably priced and consistently acceptable, clean and convenient with wheelchair access and disabled rooms plus Wi-Fi connection.
Avenue du Dauphiné, Briançon. Tel: (04) 92 20 02 00. www.ibishotel.com
L'Auberge du Choucas ££–£££

Sweetly decorated with sunny balconies and a lovely garden, this is a welcoming country retreat.
Le Monêtier-les-Bains. Tel: (04) 92 24 42 73. www. aubergeduchoucas.com
Hôtel Alliey & Résidence Le Pré des Ors ££–£££

A good-value option with a lovely spa. Half board is offered and the restaurants serve up classic dishes with gourmet twists. The residence has self-catering apartments.

11 rue de l'École, Le Monêtier-les-Bains. Tel: (04) 92 24 40 02. www.hotelalliey.com

Hôtel Valérie ££–£££

Rates are based on room-only in summer and half board in winter. The rooms are simple and classic and the ski lifts are close.

Place Montegrosso d'Asti, Montgenèvre. Tel: (04) 92 21 90 02. www.hotel-montgenevre. com

EATING OUT

Le Panier Alpin £

Indulge in a treat such as chocolate fondue alongside tea or coffee at this *salon de thé*.

48 Grande-Rue, Briançon. Tel: (04) 92 20 54 65. www.panieralpin.com

La Caponnière ££

One of six Briançon restaurants specialising in Vauban menus, La Caponnière serves up some unique local dishes. On Friday evenings, staff dress up in period costumes.

122 rue Commandant Carlhan, Petite

Gargouille, Briançon. Tel: (04) 92 20 36 77.

Le Refuge ££

Value for money and attentive staff make Le Refuge a good option.

Rue Église, Montgenèvre. Tel: (04) 92 21 92 97.

ENTERTAINMENT

Centre Astro de Briançon-Les Écrins

For an unusual evening, try observing the starry night skies at this planetarium in a hamlet near Briançon.

Bouchier. Tel: 06 75 47 77 73. www.observatoire-briancon.com (in French).

Spirit de Briançon

Bar-restaurant with comfortable lounge seating spilling out on to a large pavement area. Cocktails and other drinks are served from 4pm, tapas and snacks from 5pm, and meals in the evening.

3 place du Temple. Tel: (04) 92 50 19 97. www.spiritbar.fr

SPORT AND LEISURE

Sun Scoot

Evening snowmobile outings in Montgenèvre

and Serre-Chevalier for €70 (driving your own snowmobile), €80 (driver and passenger) or €20 (as a passenger with a guide).

Tel: (04) 92 21 83 35 (Montgenèvre) / (04) 92 24 21 70 (Serre-Chevalier). www.sunscoot.fr

Lac de Serre-Ponçon area

ACCOMMODATION

Camping Le Verger £

One of many campsites close to the Lac de Serre-Ponçon, Le Verger is open year-round and has family-size *gîtes* for hire plus tent pitches, heated pool, games areas and a bar-restaurant.

Barratier. Tel: (04) 92 43 15 87.

www.campingleverger.fr

Hôtel de la Mairie £–££

The rooms at this highly likeable town hotel vary in size, but all are bright and smart, with a fresh minimalist design. Free Wi-Fi is available. Interesting artworks decorate the communal areas.

Place Barthelon, Embrun. Tel: (04) 92 43 20 65. www.hoteldelamairie.com

Eating out
Restaurant de la Mairie ££

Attached to the hotel, the restaurant has a large outdoor area on the central town square. With several set menus, including a healthy vegetarian meal, there is plenty of choice. Round off the evening with a drink from the old-fashioned bar.

See 'Hôtel de la Mairie', p187.

Sport and leisure
Mont'Ânes

This farm organisation offers packages ranging from walking with llamas and donkeys (from €30) to weekend camping excursions with donkeys (€128 for a family of four). They also rent out camping pitches.

Le Serre, Crots. Tel: (04) 92 23 16 70. www.montanes.fr

Gap and around
Accommodation
Hôtel Le Clos £

This budget hotel just outside Gap is a good rest-stop on the famous Route Napoléon (Côte d'Azur to Grenoble), with a nice garden, restaurant and terrace.

20 avenue Commandant Dumont. Tel: (04) 92 51 37 04. www.hotel-restaurant-parc-golf.hotel-restaurant-leclos.com

Eating out
Le Tourton des Alpes £–££

Tourtons, filled fritters that are a speciality of the Gap area, can be picked up at the Saturday market, but for a sit-down meal this is the place to go.

1 rue des Cordiers, Gap. Tel: (04) 92 53 90 91. Open: lunch & dinner. Closed: outside high season Sun & Mon.

Entertainment
Le Ballardin

Billed as a café-theatre-disco-karaoke bar, Le Ballardin is a unique place to spend a Friday or Saturday evening.

3 rue de la Cathédrale, Gap. Tel: (04) 92 52 34 17. www.leballadin.com

Sport and leisure
Pegasus France

Run by a British team, this microlight school has English-speaking instructors. One-hour taster flights are available, or you can sign up for a holiday course. Minimum age 12 years.

Gap-Tallard aerodrome. Tel: 06 13 62 73 73 (Gap) / +44 (0)1577 863 645 (UK). www.pegasusfrance.co.uk

Parc National des Écrins
Accommodation
Hôtel de Plein Air Les Cariamas £–££

Charming self-catering wooden chalets with heated outdoor pool, bicycle rental, fishing lake and a calm setting close to the ski stations.

Fontmolines, Chateauroux-Les-Alpes. Tel: (04) 92 43 22 63. www.les.cariamas.free.fr

Eating out
La Farandole ££

Try salted sweet crêpes and traditional cuisine at this friendly rôtisserie with a sunny terrace.

Rond Point Pistes, Orcières-Merlette. Tel: (04) 92 43 85 31.

SPORT AND LEISURE
La Tyrolienne
Travel head first horizontally down a 870m (950-yard) long zip cable at 140km/h (87mph), a thrill available to anyone over ten, in summer and winter.
Roll'Air Cable, Orcières 1850. Tel: (04) 92 21 81 74. www.latyrolienne.fr

Alpes-de-Haute-Provence
ACCOMMODATION
Hôtel Villa Gaïa ££
Exuding elegance, this old villa has been transformed into a restful hotel. Half board is available (vegetarian options on request) and includes a soak in the wood-heated steam bath.
24 route de Nice, Digne-les-Bains. Tel: (04) 92 31 21 60.
www.hotelvillagaia.fr.
Open: mid-Apr–Oct.

EATING OUT
Auberge du Point Sublime ££
In the stunning scenery of the Gorges du Verdon, this route-side inn (which also has guest rooms) boasts an amazing view from the dining terrace.
Sur départementale 952, Rougon. Tel: (04) 92 83 60 35 / (04) 92 83 69 15. Open: Apr–Nov.

SPORT AND LEISURE
Établissement Thermal
Pampering opportunities here include treatments with a Provençal flavour (using citrus, lavender and herbs), from €55 for a combination of two treatments.
Digne-les-Bains. Tel: (04) 92 32 58 46. www.thermesdigneslesbains.com. Open: Mar–early Dec.

Mercantour area
ACCOMMODATION
Hôtel Le Gélas ££
The rooms at this cosy Logis de France hotel are designed with simple, clean lines. Information on Mercantour activities is provided and a buffet breakfast is included.
27 rue Docteur Cagnoli, Saint-Martin-Vésubie. Tel: (04) 93 03 21 81. www.hotel-vesubie.com (in French).
Lou Ben Manjà ££
At the foot of the Mercantour mountains, the télécabine to skiing in Auron is nearby. The star rating is based on half board; full board is also available.
Place San Ment, Saint-Étienne-de-Tinée. Tel: (04) 93 02 40 28. www.loubenmanja.fr (in French).

EATING OUT
Le Chamois d'Or £
Next to the marketplace in Saint-Étienne, this café-restaurant has a spacious terrace, a set savoury and sweet crêpes menu, and other simple choices including salads and ice cream.
1 avenue Charles de Gaulle, Saint-Étienne-de-Tinée. Tel: (04) 93 02 44 80.

SPORT AND LEISURE
Centre Équestre du Mercantour
Join a day trek in the national park on horseback for €60. One-hour lessons are offered for €20.
La Colmiane, Valdeblore. Tel: 06 08 99 06 11. Open: Apr–Oct daily; Sept–Oct weekends only.

Index

Acknowledgements

Thomas Cook Publishing wishes to thank DANNY LEVY SHEEHAN, to whom the copyright belongs, for the photographs in this book, except for the following images:

La Clusaz Tourist Office 15; Thea Macaulay 48, 49, 115, 135; Xenia Macaulay 28, 29, 30, 31, 35, 36, 37, 38, 40, 43; Linda Thomson 138; Val d'Isère Tourist Office 97, 150

For CAMBRIDGE PUBLISHING MANAGEMENT LIMITED:
Project editor: Jennifer Jahn
Copy editor: Anne McGregor
Typesetter: Trevor Double
Proofreaders: Jan McCann & Caroline Hunt
Indexer: Marie Lorimer

SEND YOUR THOUGHTS TO BOOKS@THOMASCOOK.COM

We're committed to providing the very best up-to-date information in our travel guides and constantly strive to make them as useful as they can be. You can help us to improve future editions by letting us have your feedback. If you've made a wonderful discovery on your travels that we don't already feature, if you'd like to inform us about recent changes to anything that we do include, or if you simply want to let us know your thoughts about this guidebook and how we can make it even better – we'd love to hear from you.

Send us ideas, discoveries and recommendations today and then look out for your valuable input in the next edition of this title.

Emails to the above address, or letters to the traveller guides Series Editor, Thomas Cook Publishing, PO Box 227, Coningsby Road, Peterborough PE3 8SB, UK.

Please don't forget to let us know which title your feedback refers to!